Becoming a Successful Illustrator

Derek Brazell and Jo Davies

Fairchild Books
An imprint of Bloomsbury Publishing Plc

50 Bedford Square   175 Fifth Avenue
London   New York
WC1B 3DP   NY 10010
UK   USA

www.bloomsbury.com

First published 2013

British Library Cataloguing-in-Publication Data
A catalogue record for this book is available from
the British Library.

ISBN
PB: 978-2940411-93-1
ePDF: 978-2940447-58-9

Bloomsbury Cataloging-in-Publication Data
Brazell, Derek and Davies, Jo.
Becoming a Successful Illustrator/Derek Brazell and
Jo Davies p.cm.
Includes bibliographic references and index.
ISBN 978-2-940411-93-1 (pbk.) –
eISBN 978-2940447-58-9 (ePDF.)
1. Commercial art.
2. Commercial art – Study and teaching.
3. Illustrators – Vocational guidance.
NC997. B739 2013

Design by Andrew Howard
Printed and bound in China

Becoming a Successful Illustrator

Derek Brazell and Jo Davies

CONTENTS

BECOMING A SUCCESSFUL ILLUSTRATOR
INTRODUCTION

The discipline of illustration is constantly expanding. It is an elastic art form which successfully stretches to wherever its varied practitioners wish to take it, illuminating text, decorating products, commenting on society, making statements as public art on walls, entertaining gamers and film viewers and persuading consumers.

As a term, illustration has evolved to embrace applications far removed from the more traditional areas of book publishing, editorial and standard print advertising, into those that may not have been recognized as illustration in the (even recent) past. Images are created for the ever-increasing number of digital platforms – apps aimed at adults and children; screen-savers and animations; designs for three-dimensional products, furniture, vinyl toys and fashion; site-specific work over the interior and exteriors of buildings and vehicles and for display. Design, motion, street art and typography are all part of illustration's growing global network, and *Becoming a Successful Illustrator* seeks to take a broad view of illustration grounding it in case studies from practitioners and commissioners from around the world.

A creative career is one that many aspire towards. The endless possibilities, independence, job satisfaction and potential for varied commissions from clients combine to create an appealing avenue of work. These attributes mean that commercial artists face much competition in the areas they choose to work in, and there are many angles to consider. Being a freelancer means you are running a business on your own as well as creating wonderful art, and therefore understanding the business side of freelance work will contribute to your success and will enable you to avoid the common pitfalls that arise in a commercial environment. Creativity is required both in your practice and in the wider context of sourcing commissions, portfolio presentations and promotion. This book will equip you, as a new professional or as a student in your final year of education, with the necessary knowledge to move forward and achieve your goals.

Becoming a Successful Illustrator is organized into clear sections covering the essential areas of working in illustration, including understanding the industry you will be working in; helping you to evaluate your skills; assessing where you may wish to apply your artwork; finding and approaching potential clients; promotion, finance, fees and your intellectual property rights. A broad range of case studies drawn from the full range of commercial art illuminate the main text, offering views and experience from seasoned practitioners and commissioners as well as more recent entrants into the field. Practical exercises at the end of the book allow you to apply what you are learning to your own experience, providing an effective base from which to launch a sustainable career in illustrative practice.

Creatives have in the past usually worked independently, either from home or a studio or in a shared rented space. However, in recent years there has been an increase in collectives of varying sizes coming together to inspire and support each other. Forging close connections with creatives working in different areas to help facilitate the aspirations of an individual can broaden artistic vision and market opportunities. For example, illustrators can work with other artists whose technical skills allow expansion into new areas. These groups create collaborative work to commission, mixing their various skills which can include animation, printmaking, typography and 3D, while maintaining parallel careers and also providing work for the individual members. They can promote the collective as an impressive one-stop-shop for clients needing a combination of skills, and this can make them an attractive option.

For an individual illustrator, employing a business partner or publicist to concentrate on promotion and financial requirements can allow time to focus on the creative aspects of the job and producing the artwork.

Historically, illustration has existed to serve a client, where the artist may have been restrained by having to follow a brief that was very specific in its scope. This is no longer the case due to the opportunities now made available through new digital avenues for marketing, retail and distribution, as well as technologies for cheap printing. These mean that illustrators are breaking free of the constraints a formal brief can impose to forge their own authorial work. Rather than personal work for its own sake this authorial output can still be successfully placed in a commercial context, such as self-published artist books/graphic novels, cards, prints, fabric designs, T-shirts, ceramics and more. This output is created with an end in mind, a step further than the investigation and pleasure that can result from purely personal creative activity. Whether authorial or purely personal it is important to recognize that work created without the possible pressures of a deadline also feeds back into commissions, maintaining essential growth over a career in illustration and design.

Becoming a Successful Illustrator offers guidance, insight, inspiring imagery from recognized talents and practical measures to help you assess your place in the image-making business and build upon it, fostering skills that will place you at an advantage in the popular field of creative commercial arts. We wish you every success.

Opposite Holly Exley, 'Teacups', watercolour painting. Illustrators can work for a range of different clients in a range of different media. Knowing where to start can be a daunting prospect!

CHAPTER ONE
ILLUSTRATION ENTERPRISE

This section will consider how you might position yourself successfully as a freelance practitioner within the professional field of illustration.

There is a distinction between creative and commercial success and just as there are steps that can be taken to develop visually, there are also strategies for developing your potential commercially. Being a talented image-maker, possessing exemplary skills as a visual communicator and having innovative ideas and means of personal expression does not guarantee a successful career as an illustrator. To succeed you will need a combination of skills, attitude and knowledge. A bit of luck is often useful too.

Gemma Latimer

UNDERSTANDING ILLUSTRATION

Although it is increasingly difficult to provide an authoritative definition of what illustration is, it is clear that there has been a shift in the boundaries of practice within the applied arts. The dissolving of traditional subject areas and increased flexibility provided by digital environments has contributed to an exciting expansion of commercial opportunities for many artists.

Illustrators no longer need to be located near to large cities with a density of publishing houses and design groups to find possible clients, nor do they need to have premises or rely on galleries to sell artworks and products. It is now commonplace for illustrators to have several forms of web presence to promote their work and finished artwork can be sent quickly and conveniently to clients anywhere around the world. Notwithstanding language barriers, the marketplace is global.

For some artists this evolution, shaped largely by new advances in technology, may be perceived as a threat to established practices. There is more visible competition and the more traditional areas of publishing and editorial avenues are in a state of flux. Having to update promotion and deliver artwork digitally adds to the workload, adding more responsibility to the artist's role.

Illustrators are generally self-employed, working on commissions for payment. Some are represented by agents who deal with most aspects of the business of operating in the field. An illustrator's product is the unique visual contribution made to an artefact, environment or experience in order to illuminate, decorate or inform.

1 Lasse Skarbövik, 'Think in a New Way', advertising campaign for Santander Bank, Norway. This image was used in animation, web, television, print and postcards. The brief was for an image representing growth and development.

UNDERSTANDING
ILLUSTRATION

WHERE DO
ILLUSTRATORS
WORK?

SKILLS IN ART AND
DESIGN

ATTITUDE

KNOWLEDGE

EVALUATING YOUR
STRENGTHS AND
WEAKNESSES

The new market is big, it's booming, and it's hungry for talent. Thanks to my ambitious publisher, the books I recently illustrated are all simultaneously launched in both Taiwan and China… Instead of lamenting the declining old market where we have seen better days, we can try to seize the golden opportunity of new markets.
Daniel Hsieh

2 Daniel Hsieh, illustration from the book *The Travels of Lao Ts'an*, published by Locus Publishing.

WHERE DO ILLUSTRATORS WORK?

3

Imagery is all around us, and increasingly, it is shifting from the most obvious applications like book jackets and T-shirts, to more subtle uses like decoration and illumination on products and advertising.

In an increasingly visual world the skills of the illustrator can be called upon for a myriad uses. Applications can be ordered into a broad range of areas, although these are flexible definitions and there will be crossover between the various areas. An illustrator will be dealing with an art director as the main point of contact for the majority of the commission types described here.

I like working across all medias and markets. At the moment, for example, I'm into fashion and wall-painting and am currently enjoying creating various ranges of scarves. Last month I also did a mural for the Diane von Furstenberg store opening and it was so much fun to get inspiration from their brand and current look and then translate that to wall painting.
Pomme Chan

3 Pomme Chan, illustrations applied to the walls, floor and ceiling of the Central Embassy, Thailand, for the 'Unfold' project.

UNDERSTANDING ILLUSTRATION

WHERE DO ILLUSTRATORS WORK?

SKILLS IN ART AND DESIGN

ATTITUDE

KNOWLEDGE

EVALUATING YOUR STRENGTHS AND WEAKNESSES

Editorial

Editorial illustration has a long tradition and although print publications are rivalled by digital platforms, illustration's ability to represent events and complex issues is still required in areas such as national and regional newspapers and their supplements and consumer magazines (women's, men's, food, gardening, travel, business-to-business and trade). Digital platforms, which may be editions of existing publications or online versions, also use illustration. The brief for this work may be dictated by the art director or come directly from reading the text that is to be illustrated. Artwork can be required at short notice and with very short deadlines – maybe a couple of days. Occasionally, turnover from generation of visuals for approval to final artwork can be a matter of hours.

Editorial illustration will accompany journalistic text, ranging from concept-based images to purely decorative pieces. It can be anything from small vignettes to double-page spreads in magazines and occasionally, although more rarely, covers for publications such as the *New Yorker* and *The Guardian*. Subject matter can include current affairs, politics, finance, lifestyle, travel, health and technology.

Cartoons are a popular element of daily news platforms with some magazines concentrating on humour and current affairs, although there are limited opportunities in cartooning.

4

I was asked to fill in as art director for The New York Times OPED page whenever the current art director was away, and I learned a great deal about the other side of illustration. Working with editors and other illustrators enhanced how I approach my job. I would see how other illustrators conducted themselves during a job and would try to emulate those who i enjoyed working with.
Wesley Bedrosian

4 Wesley Bedrosian, 'Practical Traveller', illustration for *The New York Times*. Wesley works largely within editorial illustration across all subjects including politics, technology and finance.

5 Paul Blow, 'Samaritans', work
for *The Independent* magazine.
Paul's clever conceptual
illustration is recognized in
magazines, newspapers and
advertising campaigns.

UNDERSTANDING ILLUSTRATION

WHERE DO ILLUSTRATORS WORK?

SKILLS IN ART AND DESIGN

ATTITUDE

KNOWLEDGE

EVALUATING YOUR STRENGTHS AND WEAKNESSES

Publishing

Book publishing in any form or media is a rich source of commissioned illustration. The four main areas across print-based and digital platforms are fiction, non-fiction and educational, children's books and graphic novels/comics. Artwork is commissioned for covers and interior illustrations. It can be line art or full colour, full-page images or frames for graphic novels and children's literature. Deadlines for the production of artwork will generally be long, reflecting the slower-moving nature of publishing. Commissioners will be publishing houses dealing in print and digital, from large internationals to small independents, and will also include clients who are commissioning for their own publications (self-publishing) and book packagers who develop and sell a concept on to publishers or retail outlets, such as large supermarkets.

Images for both fiction and non-fiction books can be an integral and important part of the publication.

6 Chris Moore, book cover illustration for *The Quantum Thief,* published by Orion. Chris Moore is one of the premier exponents of science fiction artwork.

7 Tom Burns, *The Ripley Trilogy,* published by The Folio Society, London. Examples of award-winning books where illustration features strongly.

7

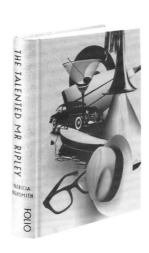

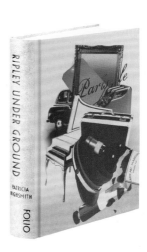

Children's books

Children's books consist of fully illustrated publications and chapter books, which will contain a smaller number of artworks – often in line – with possibly one image per chapter.

Picture books may be written by the illustrator or a separate author and are classified according to reading ages – usually baby books, toddlers and aged five to eight. Chapter books are often classified as early reader and confident readers. Illustrators need to recognize that as well as age categories, each publisher has certain types of books on its list and that the subjects covered can be seasonal.

Publishers are keen to sell second rights for children's books, so content which appeals to a potentially diverse international audience is favoured.

As producing a picture book is a lengthy and costly business and publishers produce a limited number of books per year, this is a very competitive area to seek work in. It is advised that you research the type of books that each publisher produces and be aware of their submission guidelines before approaching them.

Payment will be a one-off flat fee or royalties, which are a percentage of each sale usually based on the publisher's net receipts (what the publisher receives minus their costs for production, marketing, distribution and other expenses). Contracts for books often include subsidiary rights which cover merchandising, translation and film rights.

8

8 David Roberts, illustrations for the children's book, *Uncle Montague's Tales of Terror* by Chris Priestley, published by Bloomsbury.

Working with another author is always a great experience. Their imagination is better than mine could ever be, and this allows me to come up with ideas I wouldn't necessarily have come up with on my own. David Roberts

UNDERSTANDING
ILLUSTRATION

**WHERE DO
ILLUSTRATORS
WORK?**

SKILLS IN ART AND
DESIGN

ATTITUDE

KNOWLEDGE

EVALUATING YOUR
STRENGTHS AND
WEAKNESSES

Graphic novels and comics

Graphic novels and comics can be published in three main ways. There are publishers producing just this type of publication where illustrators work on a page rate as writers, line-artists, inkers, letterers or colourists; they usually work with recognized and licensed characters.

The second type of comic is published in the same way as other illustrated picture books. This process either involves submitting a dummy book and examples of finished artwork for consideration, or being commissioned by a publisher to create a title based on a script or idea. Some comic book artists write their own material and some work with a writer.

The third avenue for comics and graphic novels is self-publishing. Increasingly this means publishing online or producing limited edition titles to be sold through specialist fairs, independent specialist bookshops and websites.

Comic book artists need to become familiar with the range of publishers and the types of work they produce in order to focus their submissions appropriately.

9 Luke Pearson, illustrations for the comic book *Hildafolk*, published by Nobrow Press.

I have a fairly traditional comics style for the most part, but coming from an illustration background has given me a good grasp of colour palettes and design which gives them a leg up in some way. My taste and therefore my goals in illustration are a bit different but equally are affected by the things I'm learning from doing comics. It's also allowed me to build an audience in two arenas, so I've got a higher profile than if I was just doing one or the other.

Luke Pearson

Design and advertising

Images for design and advertising are usually commissioned through an agency on behalf of an end client. Corporate clients may require images for a whole range of contexts that need to perform varied functions across print and digital platforms. This can include logos, websites and intranet, brochures, newsletters, direct mail to potential customers, annual reports and in-house promotional material such as cards, posters and calendars. Clients range from multi-national organizations (trading in food, beauty, energy and commodities), government departments, entertainment producers and venues, retail outlets and small local businesses and individuals. The subject range that an illustrator may cover through design-based work is infinite.

It's been important to be able to adapt my work to fulfil the client's needs and expectations.
Stuart Kolakovic

10 Anke Weckmann, 'Max in Pocket', illustrations applied to a lip balm case for Too Cool for School cosmetics.

11 Stuart Kolakovic, skateboard design. Illustration can be applied to virtually any object.

12 Ulla Puggaard, 'Eyes Up', advertising poster for Audi A6, Audi. (Art Director Kevin Stark, Agency BBH London).

13 Karen Greenberg, images for Gevalia Columbia, Espresso Roast and House Blend coffee packaging. (Client: Landor Associates for Kraft Foods.)

13

Packaging for food, games and toys, health and beauty products will create brand identity.

Within the music business, album cover artwork for physical and online display, merchandising (T-shirts, buttons, tour posters), backdrops, promo videos, gig posters and identities for club nights and festivals across multiple platforms will become an integral part of the entertainment experience.

Advertising consists of roadside poster hoardings, building wraps and bus shelters through to adverts in magazines and newspapers and online static and animated banners.

Advertising commissions will often have short deadlines, and involve a lot of direction and approval of artwork levels.

There is often less flexibility in this area of work and less opportunity for the illustrator to have creative input.

Below-the-line advertising is work commissioned for promotional items sent directly to a specified group of people, often via post.

Illustration for screen

Illustration is increasingly prevalent in digital platforms such as the Web, games, mobile devices, television and cinema. The visual content of games for computers and mobile devices includes characters and backgrounds as well as interactive elements; all of these elements can be devised by illustrators.

Animation is generally a freelance occupation, and can encompass working on a major film, games on social media sites, advertising – both standard and viral – and apps. Motion artists may be approached by a production house to be involved with a project or they may generate their own. Television will use idents for channels and programmes, especially those aimed at a younger demographic.

When we started Problem Bob none of us had ever worked with graphics for hand-held devices like iPhone and iPad before. Coming from the traditional world of advertising and illustration we wanted to break out from the restrictions set by clients and create a mark of our own. Creating the graphics for an app or website doesn't differ that much from creating artwork for print except for the resolution, and that you work more at a pixel-based level. The client expects updates and improvements, and as hardware changes we need to change with it, so apart from shape and form and a basic knowledge of the most common design applications out there, I guess that the main qualities you need to posses are curiosity, a vivid imagination and patience.
Problem Bob

UNDERSTANDING
ILLUSTRATION

**WHERE DO
ILLUSTRATORS
WORK?**

SKILLS IN ART AND
DESIGN

ATTITUDE

KNOWLEDGE

EVALUATING YOUR
STRNEGTHS AND
WEAKNESSES

16

14, 15, 16 Problem Bob,
illustrations for the multi-
player game app for iPad, *Aces
of Steam*.

Concept artists for film

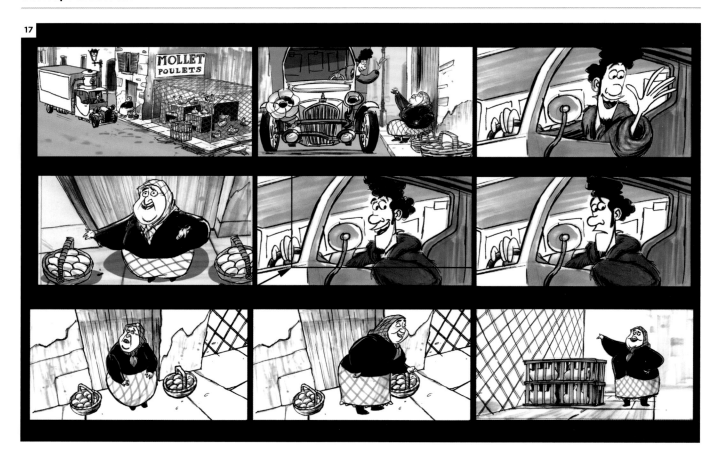

17 Matt Jones, animation storyboard for *A Monster in Paris*. Bibo Films, 2011. Distributed in the UK by Entertainment One.

Concept artists are highly specialized freelance illustrators who are usually employed in the earliest stages of a film to visualize its content, either to support bids for finance or inform the production. They usually work in teams with visual researchers and draughtsmen under the direction of the production designer, and are likely to be specialists in particular content such as creating fantastical creatures or inventing locations and scenes. There is a limited demand for work within this area with the most lucrative projects being big budget sci-fi, fantasy, or historical films.

20 Matt Jones, gesture drawings from a drawing class where illustrators draw very rapid poses (15 seconds to two minutes) and practise creating character and story from the models' poses.

UNDERSTANDING
ILLUSTRATION

**WHERE DO
ILLUSTRATORS
WORK?**

SKILLS IN ART AND
DESIGN

ATTITUDE

KNOWLEDGE

EVALUATING YOUR
STRENGTHS AND
WEAKNESSES

**You have to be familiar with
architecture, landscape and the
human form from every angle to be
able to draw storyboards or animate
traditionally. That's where maintaining
a sketchbook comes in; to help build
that repository of observation. I find
once you draw something it sticks
in the brain. The larger your mental
reference library is the easier it'll
be to draw whatever is required.
Classical life drawing is a fundamental
requirement also – the ability to really
observe and draw the human form is a
discipline that seems to be dying out.
To complement this quick 'gesture'
studies are essential too – to capture
a fleeting pose or attitude in seconds
is good practice for doing the same in
a storyboard or animation drawing.**

Matt Jones

18, 19 Stills from the film *A
Monster in Paris*, Bibo Films,
2011. Distributed in the UK by
Entertainment One.

Concept artists for games

21

Concept artists create the visual elements of a game and sometimes the graphic interface. They may also create concept art and storyboards to visualize the proposed content during the pre-production phase. Storyboard artists create drawings that demonstrate how the player progresses through the game. These are often salaried posts not freelance commissions, although increasingly these are short-term contracts.

22

Undamaged road open to a multiple vehicles to drive side by side

Earthquake causes the road to twist and crack

A heavy understanding of traditional art skills and drawing will always give you a better understanding of form and composition. It can be all too easy to use a computer package and try and let it do too many things for you, but you do need to have the understanding of lighting, form and composition and if you do, this is then very apparent in your images.

Steve Hird

21 Steve Hird, still from the game *MotorStorm Apocalypse*, produced by Evolution Studios/Sony, 2010.
22 Steve Hird, draft illustrations for the game *MotorStorm Apocalypse*, Evolution Studios/Sony, 2010.

Multiple sections of the surface collapse leaving a more narrow route

Documentary illustration

Documentary illustration can include highly researched imagery providing or recording very specific information for many purposes such as technical, historical and product visualization and may be used in many contexts including scientific, commercial and educational environments.

Reportage illustration records and comments on actual events and circumstances, and much reportage is created by drawing on location, capturing a single moment or series of events that will place the artist in the situation, adding a human observational element to the event. This can be anything, although commercial application of this type of representation of life is likely to focus on political events and characters, conflict from different perspectives, sporting events and human stories.

Opportunities for reportage work are not substantial, but art directors can recognize its power to depict a layered viewpoint of a situation or event and it can be commissioned in all the contexts where illustration is employed.

I started out doing self-contained, almost decorative illustrations but gradually changed to on-the-spot reportage drawing, which could be used in different ways and with more freedom to explore the subject matter. The skill that has been most important to me during the course of my career is the ability to twist what I want to draw into what someone wants me to illustrate. Creating opportunities for doing different sorts of work is also important.
Lucinda Rogers

23 Lucinda Rogers, 'Newspaper Seller on E 42nd Street', an observational drawing forming part of a personal collection.

24

24 Alberto Cerriteño, 'El Catrin', a poster celebrating Día de los Muertos (Day of the Dead).

UNDERSTANDING ILLUSTRATION

WHERE DO ILLUSTRATORS WORK?

SKILLS IN ART AND DESIGN

ATTITUDE

KNOWLEDGE

EVALUATING YOUR STRENGTHS AND WEAKNESSES

Decorative illustration

Technology has increasingly facilitated the move from the two-dimensional to the three-dimensional for illustration, covering a multitude of products from phone and tablet skins, stationery products, rucksacks, toys (soft and vinyl) to furniture and wallpapers.

Site-specific imagery is created for an individual location rather than multiple reproductions and will include street art on walls, vehicles (for advertising), one-off fabricated installations and in-store point-of-sale or shop window displays.

When several fashion designers approached me asking to use my illustrations in their collections it was probably the first time I saw the potential of my images being applied on products.
Catalina Estrada

Illustration for merchandising

The merchandising industry requires imagery for greetings cards, stationery, ceramics (whether functional or purely decorative), novelty items and more. Illustrators may produce surface patterns and designs for use on fabric in repeats or as individual images for garments, either mass-produced or in limited edition batches.

Illustrators are commissioned to produce designs or they may license their own specially created or existing imagery for use on various items for clients. They can also customize existing objects or create their own.

25, 26 Catalina Estrada, illustrations applied to travel bags, for Joumma Bags.

25

26

Authorial illustrators

Authorial illustrators are generators of their own material – created as a self-initiated project with no immediate commercial application, or as one which is intended to be a business endeavour. An external client is not always required to instigate a project – there has been a sizeable increase in illustrators concentrating on creating their own products to market, facilitated by the increased ease of selling items online to a potentially wide audience of consumers interested in unique handmade, artist-focused artefacts. These can be artist books, decorated garments, ceramics, individual or manufactured toys, cards, badges, hand silk-screened/ linocut prints or giclée prints from digital files.

27 Evgenia Baranova, hand-painted cup and saucer.

My style changes quite a bit from year to year, and can reflect whatever period of illustration or design history that I'm excited about at that moment. I'm also always trying out different materials and new ways of working. Despite these constant explorations, I think my illustrations all convey the same peculiar sense of character and feel, regardless of the medium or style I choose. I take on illustration work that provides an interesting graphic challenge or represents something that I admire or enjoy, and since starting as an illustrator I've made sure to stick to doing projects that I'll have fun with or will learn from in some way.
Lille Carré

28 Lilli Carré, illustrated pages from the book *Don't Drink from the Sea*, Silkscreen printed and hand-bound.

IT IS SO CROWDED TONIGHT.

ON THE HOT STREET

UNDERSTANDING ILLUSTRATION

WHERE DO ILLUSTRATORS WORK?

SKILLS IN ART AND DESIGN

ATTITUDE

KNOWLEDGE

EVALUATING YOUR STRENGTHS AND WEAKNESSES

Exhibitions are increasingly used as a way of promoting authorial work to a potential client base.

Self-generated work allows for a continued development of your artwork outside of the prescriptive constraints of a commercial project, keeping your work fresh through growth, sketchbooks and notebooks.

29 Agnès Decourchelle, illustrations from the young adult's fiction book, *Le Bonheur de Kati*, by Jane Vejjajiva, published by Gallimard Jeunesse.
30 Agnès Decourchelle, personal travel sketchbook.

**It has been important during my career that I have the ability to adopt a point of view that allows me to see things differently than others would. I've always experimented with different techniques.
Then as I grow older I get more confident in what I am doing. The experience makes the difference.**
Agnès Decourchelle

WORKING IN AN EDITORIAL ENVIRONMENT: MARCOS CHIN

The ability to capture a concept visually is beautifully conveyed by Marcos Chin in his award-winning artwork for a wide range of editorial clients. Intriguing perspectives, pleasing colourways and strong narrative elements combine to give his images an accessibility and depth which enables him to comment on subjects as diverse as gaming for girls, financial planning and legal dilemmas. 'Ideally,' he says, 'I would like to be seen as someone who enhances the text that I work with.'

Illustration wasn't a profession that Marcos was aware of until he was in the second semester of art college, but he chose that direction because 'I knew that I wanted to tell stories through my pictures for a living. Like many kids, I dreamt of drawing comics and graphic novels, but realized very early on that I didn't possess the kind of patience and commitment that an artist requires to complete such a project.'

Once he was introduced to editorial illustration it connected, as it provided the opportunity to work on various types of projects in a relatively short amount of time: 'I could be given a story about autism, and then the next day it would be a short story fiction; this is what I love most about my profession, I learn so much and am exposed to so much through the words of someone else.'

Focusing on editorial gave Marcos the opportunity to hone his craft; to strengthen his drawing and painting techniques: 'The deadlines were constant and as a result I was forced to understand the characteristic of the materials that I used, respect time (management), and I also learned very early on the importance of experimenting and failing often, recovering from those missteps, and then learning from them in order to move forward and improve as an illustrator.'

When given an assignment he will often ask the art director if he or she has any direction for him to follow. He will then sketch down as many ideas as possible: 'At this stage there are no bad ideas, everything is valid, and each idea is given space in the form of a rough thumbnail-sized sketch. Once I have spent a couple of hours on this stage, I begin to survey and analyze the thumbnails to see which ones have the potential to become a final illustration.'

He will do photo research, but at the start of the sketching process the work is based entirely on resources received from the client – text or an article: 'The research begins after I feel as though I've exhausted all of the ideas from my brain, and need some help opening my mind to new possibilities of visually interpreting an idea. Research for me means providing myself with a new way of seeing.'

An ongoing curiosity about the world and the development of his own process keeps his artwork evolving: 'My studio practice purposely includes doing things, creating objects, and exploring creative disciplines which exist outside of illustration, providing continuous challenges.'

His sense of composition adds strongly to the concept that he is illustrating; it never overwhelms the idea. This gives the viewer enough to be intrigued, thus allowing him or her to continue observing the piece and to be pulled into the article. It is an approach that marks him out from his contemporaries.

1 A Tiger's Revenge, illustration accompanying a story about the hunt for a man-eating tiger along the Russian/Chinese border, published in *Men's Journal*.
2 Hooked Up, fashion product illustration showcasing men's clothing and accessories, published in *Complex Magazine*.
3 Illustration to accompany an article on the dwindling number of pro-bono cases that lawyers in the US take on, *American Lawyer* magazine.

SKILLS IN ART
AND DESIGN

Become an octopus. Learn how to deal with your priorities in life and set a healthy but effective order for them.
Olimpia Zagnoli

You already possess either a solid body of artwork or a range of creative and technical skills you can use to build a portfolio of credible imagery that demonstrates your potential to clients. However strong your folio of work or however specialized it may be, whichever types of work are enjoying popularity, it is wise to cultivate a broad foundation of art and design skills. These include confidence in using colour, composition, drawing, and awareness of the potential of a range of materials and approaches as well as the ability to research and generate ideas to communicate through your imagery. These rudimentary skills – that are fundamental to many art and design activities – expand the potential for flexibility and possible longevity.

Having design skills and sensibilities is vital. Being aware of shifting boundaries and new possibilities is important. Cultivating an individual voice is the tip of the iceberg. It is essential that your folio shows examples of the subjects, content, approach and the contexts that you hope to work in.

Many of the traditional labels used to identify practice are now defunct and many freelance illustrators will create work that communicates in different ways because of the way in which it is applied. As a freelancer you will need to identify the openings available for your work and inspire the commissioner to be confident in your ability to fulfil a brief.

If you have not yet had commissions, producing convincing mock-ups of your work digitally can show how it could work in different formats, at differing scales and for diverse audiences. This means recognizing that images function in different ways.

31 Olimpia Zagnoli, 'The Scoop' iPhone app for *The New York Times*. As a freelancer, you will need to identify openings available for your work.

UNDERSTANDING ILLUSTRATION

WHERE DO ILLUSTRATORS WORK?

SKILLS IN ART AND DESIGN

ATTITUDE

KNOWLEDGE

EVALUATING YOUR STRENGTHS AND WEAKNESSES

Generic skills

There are some skills which are essential to practice in illustration. Being competent with digital technology as a means of communication, being conversant with the visual voc abulary of design and being able to take an image through a digital process of scanning, adjusting mode and resolution in order to post it online or to send it to a client, are considered standard requirements. Being confident within the general field recognized broadly as graphic design could also open many doors for you as a freelancer.

Most illustrators will also handle type or produce imagery that will exist within a graphic context, so being articulate with the language of typography is essential.

Having a broad visual literacy and sense of visual discernment is also desirable and this can be developed by cultivating an expansive interest in the visual arts as well as looking at the work of other illustrators, visiting exhibitions and keeping up to date with the industry by regularly reading the design press and blogs.

Transferable skills

Transferable skills are those which equip you to function and work effectively across a broad spectrum of professional, commercial and social arenas.

Being able to organize your time and resources to achieve the plethora of tasks associated with both finding work and running a business as a freelancer is essential. Whether it is being confident in communicating appropriately in verbal and written forms, confidently asserting your rights when negotiating a licence for a job, or having the skills to persuade a gallery owner to show your work, transferable skills will be vital to the successful operation of your business.

Business skills

Many creatives find it difficult to distance themselves from their work and recognize what they produce as a commodity or service. You must apply an objective and analytical understanding of the commercial potential inherent in a folio to profit from it. It's not bad taste to see creative practice as an activity whose objective is to lead to financial success.

Business skills will equip you to turn something that you enjoy into a service you offer in return for financial remuneration and to facilitate the process of it becoming a sustainable concern. You will also need to understand how to manage your finances and to deal with the very particular business of profit and loss and the practicalities of invoices, bookkeeping, taxes, insurance and financial planning and accounting.

It's important to be really organized, to have a calendar of all your deadlines, to only reply to emails at certain times of the day and to keep a master list of jobs you are working on, what projects are in what stage, what needs to be invoiced, who needs a quote, etc. It is not second nature to many, but if you don't stay on top of this stuff, it can really impact your work in a bad way.
Jessica Hische

WORKING ACROSS A RANGE OF MEDIA:
ALBERTO CERRITEÑO

'Always, a big part of what I do is to try new things and constantly experiment with new formulas to create my work,' states Mexican illustrator Alberto Cerriteño, on working across a broad range of illustration areas. 'I need to stay engaged and interested with what I do, and sometimes the only way to do that is by using a totally new media. An inspiration for approaching different techniques comes from observing other artists' work. It makes me challenge myself in a very exciting way.'

Having worked across design and animation as well as image-making, Alberto believes his illustration style is the result of many years of being a graphic designer, applying basic design rules, such as colour, form, line and composition. 'Those rules are pretty much applied all the time in my illustrations, providing them with a better visual balance.' His animation experience also builds into 2D work. 'I believe the expression and poses of my static images in some way reflect animation, because I think in motion; little sequential stories come to my mind when I'm sketching a new project.'

Although Alberto's artwork has been applied across motion work, skins for mobile devices and even puppets for a video, he does not actively seek out different areas to utilize his work, although he's not afraid to try new areas when the opportunity is presented. 'I feel excited when I get the chance to apply my illustrative creations in a different media or discipline outside the typical 2D. Sometimes the big challenge is trying to preserve my style across the projects when they're not 2D, but that's the gasoline that keeps me going with the project – to learn new things and become more diverse in my execution.'

The illustration process continues to be an enjoyable one for him. 'It is a discipline that allows me to do what I personally enjoy the most, on a professional basis,' he says, 'so illustration for me is a dream come true.' The big challenges are when he is outside of his comfort area, 'meaning when I need to execute something I'm not used to', and if he finds himself struggling to come up with fresh ideas, 'what works for me is to leave the paper for a moment and do anything not related to the work I'm doing, I guess just clearing my mind with a little distraction helps to unclog the drain.'

Alberto approaches the business side of illustration seriously. Although he used to create work specifically for self-promotion, he now finds the Internet has become a great free promotional tool. 'I try to keep my work posted on the various social media sites that you can find out there, and in my personal experience it's the best and cheapest way to be in many places.' He sells prints and licenses artwork for consumer products, and invests time on that side of his business. 'It's been working really well, and I have plans to continue and even increase those business initiatives. We are living in a great moment now where people are getting more and more interested in acquiring affordable art in many forms.'

1 Illustrations used in the music video to Brian Vogan's children's song That's how a Pumpkin Grows'. Animated by FashionBuddha.
2 Packaging for INQ Social Mobiles.
3 Creating characters for a video series, featuring hand-crafted puppets. In collaboration with FashionBuddha.

2

3

ATTITUDE

Every illustrator wants to be successful – to have a long career doing fulfilling work for interesting clients, whilst earning a good living. At different times in your career, this ambition will be shaped by various factors. In the early stages, lack of experience of dealing with clients will be compensated for by enthusiasm and energy. Having to do other part-time work whilst building up regular or well-paid work may be imperative. Later on, the demands may stem from keeping up-to-date with new technologies or fitting freelance work around the particular demands of family life.

It's important to nourish your desire to create and express ideas: if you are passionate about illustration and genuinely engaged with the creation of imagery or artefact, you are more likely to have the right attitude to survive.

Just as having an openness to experiment and learn underpins much creative enterprise, having openness about what you can apply your skills to commercially will make the possibilities available to you seem greater. This means considering all options and assessing opportunities to see how you can profit from them in the short or long term.

When you are building a business, sometimes the gains are not immediately financial but may strengthen your profile, contribute to developing your network or gaining more experience or skills. Being honest about what you can possibly achieve and realistic about your ambitions is important, as well as tenacity and adaptability if success isn't immediate.

Becoming businesslike

As a freelancer you are often alone with your folio in a world that can appear vast, dynamic and challenging. Before approaching potential clients, you should evaluate what you offer and conduct an honest self-appraisal in the light of what the market needs. This is the equivalent of any other micro-business or service provider doing an audit of stock or a larger company matching a potential employee against a person specification for a job opportunity. You also need to be confident that you will be able to deliver what you are offering.

You can begin defining yourself as an illustration entrepreneur by understanding what you have to offer, who will buy it and for how much. This understanding is a good foundation for your business.

Ask yourself some simple questions before launching out into your career. Here is a sample but not inexhaustible list of things to consider:

Questions about your product
— What is my product?
— What is the unique selling point that I have as an illustrator?
— Who are my competitors?
— How strong is my product compared to theirs?

Questions about the market
— Who will buy what I make?
— Where will I find these potential clients?
— How will I sell my product to them?
— How much could I earn from this?

Practical questions
— How economically viable is my product?
— Do I want or need to invest in developing my product?
— Do I enjoy making it?
— Have I the resources to make this product?

32

IL MERLO LUIGI FASOT 'SVENTO' LA MISTERIOSA E INVISIBILE MINACCIA CHE SI ABBATTE' SENZA DANNI A BENI, ANIMALI E PERSONE IN OGNI ANGOLO DELLA CONTRADA. NEL TERZO LUSTRO I CITTADINI POSERO MDCCCLXXX

32 Paolo Rui, 'History 8 – 1865 The Invisible Menace', acrylic painting on canvas. Paolo is the president of the European Illustrators Forum.

One of the first things an illustrator should learn when starting a career and should always keep in mind is that we are all unique, but replaceable, and, no matter how good we can get, there are scores of others ready to wear our shoes. This is called competition, but that must not be synonymous with accepting cheaper fees or worse contracts in order to get a job; on the contrary, competition should be a positive force to make us progress in both the artistic field as much as in the way we are able to communicate with our clients and discuss the terms of the agreements under which we are going to work.

Paolo Rui

WORKING ACROSS THE FIELD OF ILLUSTRATION: BEN NEWMAN

Ben Newman is an illustrator working seamlessly across diverse areas of art practice. His artwork contributes to the evolving definition of illustration through its application across various formats, including commissioned and authorial work.

Ben explains that his love of illustration practice comes from the opportunity to operate within the grey areas of both fine art and graphic design. 'Illustration can sometimes move closer to ideals and practices in fine art, and then in other circumstances it can supply the same problems and solutions as graphic design.' He has never considered illustration to be just editorial work or pictures for children's books, as 'it can encompass such a huge range of our everyday, which lots of people don't notice because they take it for granted. I've had the opportunity to work in product design, advertising, interior design, sculptures, comics, book jacket design and international exhibitions.' He believes that his ability to work fluidly over these different areas derives from a strong, unique creative voice that isn't afraid to keep evolving or to fail.

Although always considering himself to be an illustrator, he says he is finally starting to appreciate the term 'artist' a lot more. 'I like to work commercially for clients and help create solutions for them but I also take great pride and enthusiasm in my own personal work. I'd like to consider myself a graphic artist as I feel this incorporates both sides of what I strive to accomplish.'

The biggest challenge he often faces is visually solving a problem for a client. 'Working up an idea from scratch that will eventually help communicate or reinforce an idea with a simple, conceptually and aesthetically pleasing image is very difficult', he says, acknowledging that this is something all illustrators battle with throughout their careers. Working over a large range of areas can create problems for Ben with consistency, 'Some jobs are a real struggle to adapt yourself and your aesthetic to, but the way to overcome this is to stay true to creative vision and to be positively responsive to criticism and seek collaboration.'

To operate successfully, Ben has developed a breadth of skills, a pragmatic approach to the organization of his time and resources as well as a positive attitude to the external forces on his work. A flexible routine is very important to his practice: 'Self discipline is the key factor in keeping your routine, as I spend a lot of time working by myself and need to stay focused on my deadlines and managing other side projects.' Key physical components for him are simple things like a pencil, ruler, eraser and the computer. 'It may sound silly but I like to work very simply, as I find that by placing restrictions on myself I create more interesting work.'

For illustrators, he considers the best skills to be having a keen eye for composition, a genuine enthusiasm for solving problems, a willingness to accept failure mixed with a lot of tenacity and a love of drawing.

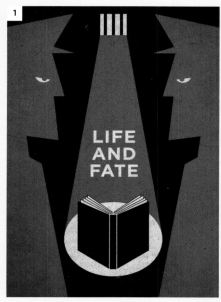

1 Poster for a BBC Radio 4 dramatization of Vassiy Grossman's *Life and Fate*.
2 Portrait of Sir Peter Cook for the '75 Peters' exhibition (2011).
3 'MASK 2', personal work.
4 'Bishop's 'o'o', work for the 'Ghost Of Gone Birds' exhibition (2011).

KNOWLEDGE

For an illustrator at the early stages of a career – independent of an agent or publicist – having knowledge of how the professional field operates is as much a prerequisite as a robust visual language, appropriate skills and an enterprising attitude. You will need to know how to find and approach clients, what kind of promotional materials are most successful and how to deal with finances. These areas will be covered in later sections of this book.

Knowing how other illustrators work, identifying what is being commissioned by whom, when and where can help you to understand how and where your own work could be commissioned. Because illustration is an accessible, ubiquitous art form present at magazine stands, in bookshops, advertising hoardings and in commercial and entertainment environments, researching the market is not a difficult task.

Although an awareness of what the market wants, what is current or what is achievable can influence how your own visual language develops, it is inappropriate and unethical to emulate another's style. An understanding and knowledge of the ethics and rights which are the foundation of the profession is therefore imperative.

Marketability is an accurate but ambiguous answer to the question of what skills and expertise are important. That can mean pure talent and technical excellence, intelligent lateral thinking or whimsy, the zeitgeist 'cool' factor and whether there's an actual need in the industry for that kind of work. A good agent can spot a potential star, based on these various measurable criteria and knowledge of the marketplace, and just plain old experience and intuition.

The personality of the individual plays an important role as well. Professional, dynamic, enthusiastic, efficient, pleasant folk, who take their career very seriously, but don't take themselves too seriously, definitely have an advantage.

This goes without saying, but it helps to have some business acumen too, and there are lots of courses available to equip one with the necessary basic tools and knowledge.
Louisa St Pierre

UNDERSTANDING ILLUSTRATION

WHERE DO ILLUSTRATORS WORK?

SKILLS IN ART AND DESIGN

ATTITUDE

KNOWLEDGE

EVALUATING YOUR STRENGTHS AND WEAKNESSES

Where do you want to work within the field of illustration?

It is important to identify those illustrators who are your competitors and to understand why they are successful. Identifying appropriate audiences, measuring the potential market to understanding what function the creative work will perform, and how potential clients could define and locate it, will help you to position yourself commercially.

It may be initially a challenge to see where you will begin working within this vast spectrum of practice, but referring to and evaluating the work of your competitors – those successful illustrators doing the kind of work that you would like to do yourself – will help you to gauge the viability of your own work. This is part of building your knowledge base about the market and how it currently operates.

Through constantly looking at agents' websites, source books, competition winners, the art and design press, current exhibitions and key illustration sites, you will familiarize yourself with what styles, content and approach are current and be able to consider where you could possibly fit into the market.

Illustrators' websites and blogs reveal useful information about the ways in which they approach their marketing and promotion and you can even contact them directly with questions that could assist you in your own career.

Illustration is a competitive and demanding profession requiring a diversity of skills and expertise. Understanding the areas in which it is commissioned and being realistic about where you may be positioned within the market is important as you embark upon your career as a freelance illustrator.

33

33 A selection of specialist magazines for illustrators.

EVALUATING YOUR STRENGTHS AND WEAKNESSES

Most contemporary illustration is encountered and presented to an audience in the following categories:

- print-based
- digital environment
- site-specific
- artefact

As what constitutes the practice of illustration within these platforms continues to expand, the range of skills which are important for you to possess also expands commensurately.

Although it would be wrong to suggest that there is one set of absolute skills that every illustrator must possess, operating across platforms and within diverse contexts does require the possession of a broad range of technical, aesthetic, personal and business skills which you will need to continue to adapt and develop in the face of changing professional challenges.

For clarity these skills can be categorized into three groups:

1. Subject specific skills – the art and design skills required in whichever area of illustration you operate within.

2. Generic skills – general skills useful for other career areas.

3. Specialist skills – additional skills specific to particular areas of practice.

Styles come and go – the way you process the information is key and will sustain a career – it's important to be creatively open-minded. Ideas never go out of fashion.

If you intend to navigate a path into the art and design industry and enjoy a long career, you should aim to develop an appropriate and evolving range of skills.

A skillful but mediocre artist won't automatically become a commercially successful illustrator. Equally, irrespective of the skills, knowledge and experience you have to offer, over the span of a freelance career some periods may be more commercially successful than others and this is the nature of self-employment for many professions.

Honestly evaluating your strengths and weaknesses and having an action plan in place will help you take a pro-active approach to developing new skills and build your confidence. Building goals into your work plan will ensure that you are focused and see periods when you don't have commissions as opportunities to be productive and to develop your practice.

Apart from specialist university and college modules and programmes, many part-time classes and online tutorial courses are available offering varying degrees of specialist content that can help you to skill up across all areas. There are also many excellent books dealing with subject-specific skill areas such as creating dummy books for children, comic books, storyboarding , drawing for fashion and concept art as well as general publications covering generic and transferable skills such as those outlined on pages 160–163.

On a personal level graduate illustrators need ambition, energy, confidence and a willingness to tackle any job and perseverance to keep going when others fall away. On a professional level it's knowledge of your market, an ability to network – telling everyone what you do and what you want and having the portfolio of work to back up your claims. What about talent? That helps, but on its own won't get you there. Luck – but as the adage goes – you make your own luck through hard work and being ready with your work.
Ashley Potter, Plymouth University, UK

UNDERSTANDING ILLUSTRATION

WHERE DO ILLUSTRATORS WORK?

SKILLS IN ART AND DESIGN

ATTITUDE

KNOWLEDGE

EVALUATING YOUR STRENGTHS AND WEAKNESSES

34

35

34, 35 Ashley Potter, stills from the official London Olympic 2012 mascot animated film, *Rainbow to the Games*. Ashley's role as production designer for the film enabled him to take on three of his undergraduate students as assistants.

CHAPTER TWO
THE PROFESSIONAL WORLD OF THE ILLUSTRATOR

Chapter 1 has revealed the broad areas in which you may typically find illustration commissions, but there will be others that the tenacious creative will be able to discover. It pays to maintain a broad outlook, keeping alert to all possible avenues of income. Don't limit yourself to what appears to be the easiest route, as this could result in a low level of commissions. Now that you have evaluated your strengths and identified areas that you can improve upon, you are in a realistic position to build on your ambitions for an expansive client list.

It's important that you learn what it means to be a professional illustrator and how to work with clients. Developing an enterprising attitude towards finding potential avenues for your work and building a robust network of professional contacts is more likely to make your career sustainable and long-lasting.

Thereza Rowe

YOUR COMMISSIONERS

Potential clients and projects range across a large spectrum: from a design firm with offices around the world creating a new brand for a global company, to an individual who is looking for someone to illustrate a children's book they have spent years writing.

This range can mean that you are approached with consummate professionalism, or that you have to deal with someone who either has little experience of commissioning illustration or who considers the illustrator to be lucky to be asked to contribute to a project. In all business circumstances your response to your clients reflects on both you and your profession. Thorough attention to the detail of a brief, patience, a businesslike approach to your communications with the client and the financial aspects of the job mark you out as a professional person to work with. This may be testing when faced with a client who is not behaving the same way, but your business dealings and professionalism will benefit from always being applied, even when you feel you are not being treated with the same respect you are offering.

Finding the right clients

- Be realistic about the type of work you can do.
- Don't get precious about the nature of the work.
- Don't rely on one client.
- Be creative about how and where your work can be used.

Regular commissions are the goal of every visual artist, and achieving a flow of work should be approached in a methodical manner. Increasingly, illustrators are working across many disciplines, but there may be certain types of clients who you are unlikely to receive commissions from if your work does not suit their business. This is where assessing your place in the market, and the areas where you might achieve success, becomes important.

Actively seeking a flow of smaller commissions will be as beneficial to your cash flow as holding out for occasional large jobs. Not every commission that you are offered will be exactly what you want to do, or offer the creative outlet you desire, but all of them help build your experience and professionalism. A realistic attitude will protect against disappointments.

Having a client who gives you repeat business is never guaranteed, though regular work can be a confidence booster as well as welcome financial support. Complacency can sometimes arise in this situation and should be guarded against. A number of commissioners can ensure an ongoing income and will also act as a barrier against the loss of a regular client. The freelancer must build into their work practice a constant search for potential new work through research and effective self-promotion, even when times are good.

Finding the right areas

The illustration industry is often fast moving and key people in your network can change roles and move on in their own careers, sometimes in new directions. If you have built up a relationship with a client, they might take you with them and this might open new doors, but the impact of new art editors or economic forces on the flavour and attitude towards commissioned illustration within a company that you have worked for can be radical.

It is natural to be drawn to an area you feel an affinity to, but being aware of the breadth of the market is going to be essential if you are to maximize your potential reach. Exploring in depth the field you wish to be involved in is logical, whether it is app games, decorative design or children's books, but considering where else your interests could be applied and seriously investigating those outlets can expand your employability. Decorative work can expand beyond greetings cards to bags, fabrics and wallpapers. Fashion illustration can be applied to garments, lifestyle editorial imagery and areas of book publishing and advertising. Graffiti also can make potent advertising – as well as specific event imagery – and is increasingly moving into gallery spaces.

1 Tad Carpenter, a poster commissioned by MTV to illustrate two of their company's core values. The illustrations were used on MTV goods such as journals, posters and other accoutrements.

1

PROFESSIONALISM

Whichever area of illustration you begin to look towards for work you should aim to cultivate a broad professional outlook and adopt an appropriate manner throughout the operation of your business.

There are some fundamental expectations which are implicit, if not stated about your role. Firstly, that you understand the briefing process and are able to deliver the services which you advertised, according to the clients' needs (we will deal with the legal dimensions of the transaction in a later section). Secondly, that you will take responsibility in the creation of the artwork that is commissioned.

In the studio situation, you can simulate 'real' briefs which allow you to produce images to function as illustrations within identified contexts and to produce mock-ups as outlined previously. Being commissioned to do this for real involves additional processes and transactions such as communicating with the client to take the brief and negotiating your rights and fees. Some of these situations can also be simulated or acted out; role play can be a valuable way of practising some of the dialogues around briefing and negotiating fees. These are specific aspects of professional practice that will be covered in later chapters. Feeling confident in these processes and bringing a consistency to the quality of how you operate as an illustrator demands a particular attitude and approach that is pivotal to professionalism.

Reliability

Although illustration can seem like a solitary activity, you are actually working in an extended team – your client, their colleagues, their organizational client, the printers. A network is established and your contribution has an impact on this bigger mechanism. Whether it's through keeping to deadlines or ensuring the quality of your artwork, weaving reliability into your profile is essential for building and maintaining professional relationships.

Good communication

Each client will communicate with you in their own way. It's likely that the phone call or email offering you a commission may seem casual and informal and the dialogue friendly. Your aim as an illustrator is to respond appropriately whatever the approach and to develop an ongoing professional rapport with each client. Good communication should be two way – whether informing existing or potential clients of recent work or keeping your client informed of the progress of ideas for a specific commission, recognizing when you need to make contact, and how to do so, is a prerequisite of the job.

2 Paul Buckley, a poster for Emzin Institute of Creative Production. Paul Buckley is Vice President Executive Creative Director at Penguin USA.

Professionalism is being able to understand a brief and not deviate from it, being honest with the timing, keeping to deadlines and giving notice as early as possible of any issues... and a friendly personality.
Choi Lui, art buyer
M&C Saatchi

Professionalism is being pleasant to work with, being into it and meeting deadlines.
Paul Buckley,
Penguin Group USA

YOUR
COMMISSIONERS

PROFESSIONALISM

JOURNALISTIC
AWARENESS

HOW TO CONTACT
POTENTIAL
CLIENTS

Confidence

Every professional illustrator has to have their first ever commission. Although in the early days of your career you may feel like a novice, it's worth remembering that through inviting you to undertake a commission for money, the client is automatically placing upon you a professional status – you have been selected, which in itself is an endorsement of your authority to undertake the job. Be confident because confidence instills confidence. This means taking responsibility for pursuing opportunities, negotiating contracts, pushing the best solution to a creative problem and being firm when appropriate.

Remember, however, that there is a distinction between confidence and arrogance.

Being calm

In the early stages of your career you may be desperate for work, but don't succumb to pestering or harassing potential clients. Being assertive is not the same as being aggressive, pushy or manipulative.

Being approached for work is exciting and given the competitive nature of the profession you may feel overwhelmed, but try to avoid responding to commissions by appearing subservient. It is important that you establish the tone of your working relationship early on.

Each commission brings its own challenges and being prepared for sudden demands or unanticipated hitches in the process, whilst maintaining composure when resolving or overcoming them, is integral to your role and essential for professionalism. A client needs to feel confident that you are capable of achieving what is asked – signs of anxiety or hysteria can be off-putting!

Information is out there and can be accessed in many ways, such as following a trail of other people, networking and talking to other creatives about their experiences, referring to client listings, utilizing trade associations and following web-based sites and magazines which focus on the broad trends in art and design.

Apart from the learning you will personally gain from working commercially, you can also learn from how other professionals operate and by keeping abreast with current news in the areas you are interested in.

You'll need to be assertive at times. Remember that as well as being in competition with other illustrators, you are also part of a community of creatives. Be well informed about what's fair in the industry in terms of fees and contracts and stand your ground. It's important to keep a good balance of being sympathetic to the needs of your client and flexible when it's appropriate, without undermining the industry.
Anna Steinberg

3

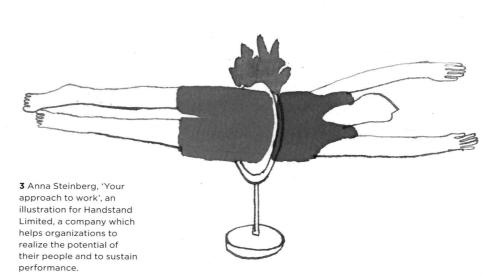

3 Anna Steinberg, 'Your approach to work', an illustration for Handstand Limited, a company which helps organizations to realize the potential of their people and to sustain performance.

JOURNALISTIC AWARENESS

Being aware of topical news within the broader industry we operate within including, but not limited to, the art and design industry is important for illustrators. Whatever your own interest there will be specialist publications: journals, magazines, papers and blogs, associated with those 'trades', be it textiles, bookselling, interior design, advertising or graphic design. The constant demand for fresh content means that there is often an editorial focus on current activities. Being aware of what's new (case studies, new campaigns) will help you keep your finger on the pulse – being able to appraise trends and predict futures is advantageous. Studying the work of those illustrators who win awards and competitions, as well as appreciating the achievements of key respected professionals, will help you gauge standards of excellence and develop your sense of visual discernment.

After university I moved to Bristol and met a lot of people, a lot of established illustrators and artists. I never once thought I was networking... but through meeting people I met other people and heard of interesting opportunities. It's good to be surrounded by people at different stages in their careers.
Rob Hodgson

Site-based venues

As exhibitions become increasingly important sources of exposure for illustrators, being aware of possible venues and the nature of shows, through guides and listings, can be profitable. Visiting local venues which show work as a sideline can also lead to new opportunities and provide inroads to niche audiences.

Illustrators' groups, subject associations, workshops and cooperatives

Meeting other experienced professionals, whatever the context, can be one of the most enjoyable – as well as reliable – ways of gaining insider industry information. Whether through more formal events such as seminars, conferences, launches, fairs and conventions or by hanging out in bars populated by advertising professionals, interaction is the best mechanism for gaining first-hand news of what is current and for making connections valuable to your network.

4 Rob Hodgson, 'Three Sisters', one panel from a mural commissioned by Plymouth County Council, as part of a city regeneration project.

4

YOUR
COMMISSIONERS

PROFESSIONALISM

**JOURNALISTIC
AWARENESS**

HOW TO CONTACT
POTENTIAL
CLIENTS

5

VAROOM!

THE ILLUSTRATION REPORT

"Anyone who tries to make a distinction between education and entertainment," said entertainer and educator Marshall McLuhan, "doesn't know the first thing about either." In this issue, stroke your chin with Sigmund Freud's Wolf Man Case Study as a graphic novel, smile at the Oscar-winning animation and peek through your fingers as illustrators tightrope-walk across the deadline of doom. "A courier arrives with a brown envelope and he is back to collect it after 2 hours, the same happens for each film. My neighbour thought that I had become a drug dealer." Noma Bar on creating the acclaimed BAFTA awards images.

AOI Association of illustrators | SUPPORTED BY **CASS ART, LONDON** | *ILLUSTRATION, CULTURE, SOCIETY* | www.varoom-mag.com

ILLUSTRATION BY STEPHAN WALTER

VAROOM! Issue 18 Spring 2012 £5

5 Stephan Walter, illustration on the cover of *Varoom*, The Illustration Report, Issue 18, 2012.

Digital networks

As agents are driven to constantly publicize the successes of the artists they represent, their blogs are a reliable source of what's happening across the industry as well as revealing what sort of work is being commissioned and by whom.

Specialist illustrators' forums and professional social networking sites are valuable platforms for presenting questions, ideas or dilemmas and to invite responses from relevant quarters.

Although the content of other illustrators' professional blogs varies in content, tone and depth, they can often be a useful way of tapping into the work lives of other practitioners. Valuable information can be gained about the range of clients, diversity of output, problems encountered and successes achieved. Following other illustrators' links can help you to extend your own industry network.

Given the openness of communication and the accessibility of illustrators via websites, you may also be able to obtain information or advice by respectfully contacting them directly.

6 Homepage for the Jacky Winters Group blog,
www.jackywinter.com.
7 A page from Jessica Hische's website,
http://jessicahische.is/
thinkingthoughts.

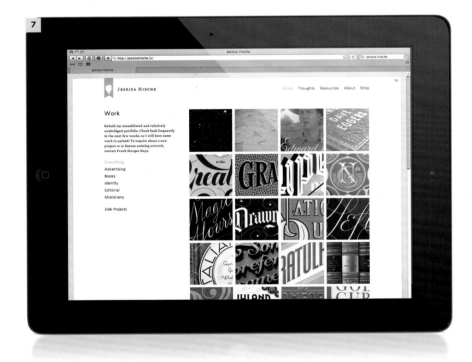

YOUR
COMMISSIONERS   PROFESSIONALISM   **JOURNALISTIC
AWARENESS**

HOW TO CONTACT
POTENTIAL
CLIENTS

Specialist trade associations and groups

Although there can be prerequisite requirements and costs involved in joining specialist trade associations and societies, the benefits to be gained through the information and advice they are able to provide can make membership an investment. Many organizations offer workshops, host events and introduce you to a wider community, as well as keeping you abreast of industry developments and providing links to associated services and information.

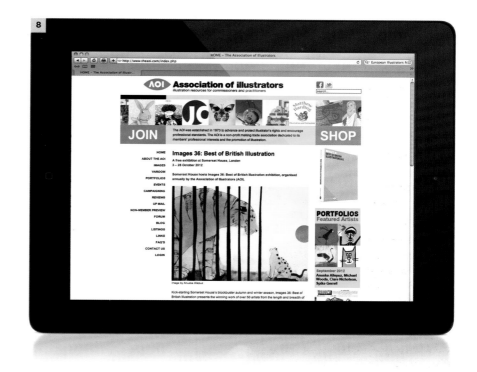

8 Homepage for the Association of Illustrators, www.theaoi.com.

Most of the problems that illustrators face in their trade are due to a general lack of awareness of some basic rules which professional associations such as those who are part of the European Illustrators Forum work hard to disseminate. Being part of one of them is a long-term investment in one's peace of mind, because, as Anita Kunz says, 'illustration more than a job is a lifestyle' and prevention is better than cure.
Paolo Rui

FINDING MARKETS FOR YOUR WORK: **WOODY**

Zara Wood, aka Woody, is an enterprising and dynamic artist whose work defies definition, whilst having huge illustrative impact. Throughout her career she has repeatedly explored the markets that exist for her work, moving beyond obvious clients to establish new outlets.

Her background in fine art equipped her with a broad set of tools which she uses to work in diverse directions, overlapping between product design, fashion, textiles and graphics. Working as a PA in advertising early in her career allowed her to see the possibilities for illustration and she began to do self-initiated projects alongside her day job. Exhibiting these in a niche London art bookshop led to a feature in their magazine *Graphic* and that subsequently led to editorial work and book cover commissions in Italy. This work led to her creation of the high-profile Star Gaze collection for Topshop, which remains one of their bestselling artists' ranges. It's important to recognize that for her the market isn't for any one product or style but for an approach. Whatever the format of the final outcome there is a strong identity in Woody's work – storytelling is a defining factor and whatever the functional application of her images, the insistence on narrative and characters that evoke an emotional connection are ingredients which Zara brings to each piece. She explains the importance of this from her own perspective:

'The narrative provides a context for my settings and characters. If the characters are believable within this context, then this acts as a form of quality control check for me.'

She is an example of someone for whom taking risks has reaped rewards. Giving up stability and moving to Australia in the early days of her career was invigorating and galvanized her ambition to be an illustrator: 'Living and working in Melbourne gave me confidence, experience and a new-found enthusiasm for illustration as a career. I did freelance commissions as well as creating art and hand-made products which were sold in independent shops.'

She stresses that retaining creative freedom is integral to her practice and the fine art sensibility she brings to her work is evident through the fluid transcending of media or material barriers. An example of this is her highly successful, self-initiated 'Little Treasures' range of jewellery – miniature artwork encased in antique lockets and pocket watches. Her work attracted a lot of influential press coverage, which showed an entrepreneurial individual open to new challenges. Although from the outside this aspect of her practice may not seem directly connected to more traditional illustrative applications, it is evidence of the benefit of not allowing yourself to be typecast or pigeon-holed.

Woody combines such authorial work with commissions where the relationship with the client is based on collaboration; working with them to produce the best solutions to briefs.

1

Although Woody's public profile increased greatly because of the work she created for big name fashion clients, she constantly creates new avenues for what she wants to do, acknowledging, 'lots of illustrators have incredible work which they advertise on blogs and websites, but you have to get people to that window.' The stationery products she created in the early days are a good example of how to find inroads into the market – to make money whilst also advertising. Finding boutiques to stock her illustrative products brought her the opportunity to both earn revenue from sales and to simultaneously gain exposure.

Woody is an excellent example of an artist who optimizes every situation. Whether writing press releases for a show, attracting interest from the design press or using social networking sites – it's a two-way process of finding out what is out there and being seen. She applies the same creative energy that instills her work to create new work opportunities. 'For me as a practitioner I'm always trying to be progressive, it's always been a critical part of sustaining my career.'

1 'Little Treasures' wearable art. Miniature art is framed within vintage jewellery.
2 'The Duchess', a three-colour screenprint on mirrored paper stock for 'Mirror Mime' exhibition at Yorkshire Sculpture Park, 2010.
3 Exhibition merchandise for the 'Mirror Mime' exhibition at Yorkshire Sculpture Park, 2010.

HOW TO CONTACT POTENTIAL CLIENTS

Industry flux and shifting of personnel within companies means that it can be difficult to find reliable up-to-date and finite compendiums which can be trusted to contain accurate contact information.

Ultimately, compiling your own database of contacts, which should be constantly revised as you gain more first-hand experience of working with clients and companies, will be the most reliable ongoing source of information.

Positioning yourself amongst other professionals

Illustration exists in many formats and places and you must establish strategies to gain equivalent exposure and be seen in similar ways to your competition. Marketing your work is an essential dimension of your professional role and to market successfully you need to recognize appropriate markets.

In the early stages of your career it is likely that you will make a substantial investment in advertising. In order to optimize the impact of this, you will need intelligent planning to target the appropriate people and places. This entails noting key names of companies and then finding job titles and contact details for individual commissioners. Find out what people's individual responsibilities are as it is likely that in larger institutions, where jobs are specialized, employees will have very specific roles and duties, which may limit the potential value they have to your career.

Looking beyond the obvious clients

When researching potential clients it is tempting to look no further than those who are easily noticed – the magazines and publishers who consistently make striking use of illustration, the high-profile brands tapping into the youth market with up-to-the-minute imagery – but most of your fellow creatives will be focusing on the same users. Each of these high-profile commissions will be mirrored in their application and uses by a multitude of lesser known equivalents. To work for an international chain of coffee houses where your imagery may be used as murals, packaging, window displays, seasonal advertising and menu design around the world would be for many a dream job. There will be smaller chains and independent coffee shops that may either approach you to undertake similar kinds of commissions or that you can approach directly with a proposal. The esteem and financial payment may not be so great, but you may be able to trade that for greater creative input and freedom and an opportunity to get your work seen.

Finding contacts for potential clients can be a chore. The AOI publish some great client directories which are really helpful. Other than that, look at every magazine, book and website that uses illustration, dig deep and try and find commissioners' names and research contacts for them.
Tom Jay

9 Tom Jay, illustration for an article about continual personal development, *Institute for Learning* magazine.

YOUR
COMMISSIONERS   PROFESSIONALISM   JOURNALISTIC
AWARENESS

HOW TO CONTACT
POTENTIAL
CLIENTS

The local market

Beyond the obvious commissioners are a host of people requiring imagery, such as smaller publishing houses and magazines producing content for a niche audience. Many organizations publish magazines for their members – cultural institutions such as museums and large galleries, unions and motoring organizations. Some of these publications are harder to find and may not be available on book stands, but as many publishing houses or groups deal with several titles, finding details for one can be a lead into multiple publications.

Walk down the high street and take note of the major stores and finance corporations; in addition to the public orientated artefacts associated with the promotion and distribution of their products and services, it is possible that there will be additional materials produced for internal distribution.

If your work is appropriate for these contexts, it is worthwhile ringing through to large corporations or service providers to see if you can make direct contact with their design department or in-house design team, if they have one, or to find out where their design work is undertaken. Check with all your friends and relatives to see if there are internal publications that they receive in their work environment, or if they are in situations where they are given illustrated materials. Corporate materials, including corporate reports and below-the-line advertising, health information brochures and law guides, are all typical examples of this type of targeted and limited distribution design.

As well as the larger corporate and commercial avenues, consider independent shops and restaurants, music and arts festivals and theatre productions, historical attractions and service providers as potential clients. They will all be looking for an individual approach and ways to draw in custom. It may be necessary to take more control in these situations, but there can be many advantages in combining work of this nature with commissions from larger scale clients.

The digital environment has created a global marketplace but it is also important that you maximize the potential of the geographical area in which you live and work. Being aware of the needs and structure of the local community may provide leads for possible direct approaches and enable you to make a name for yourself as a specialist or expert.

As well as making yourself known to all the recognized avenues for illustration – local design groups, advertising agencies, publishers and galleries – this may also entail finding other possible outlets to both show and sell your work, such as craft fairs and niche bookshops. A local setting may provide greater opportunities to recognize gaps in the market which you can exploit, and a chance to approach potential clients directly.

Individual clients

Taking a proactive approach may result in convincing a potential client of the benefits to their business in utilizing unique imagery. A local fashion shop may benefit from hand-painted window displays, a café could profit from specially illustrated menus, or the drab website of a certain business might be enlivened by an animated banner promoting their wares more effectively.

Being contacted by an individual looking to commission artwork can result in a fruitful collaboration, but there are points to be aware of in these situations:

Pros	Creative freedom	Greater input to the process	Possibility of being involved with a venture that may grow	Potential for the positive exposure for your work	Opportunity to exchange skills

Cons	Financial rewards may be minimal	May require high levels of involvement	Could be risks that the job doesn't go into production	Probable that client may not be aware of your rights as an illustrator	

Clients with a limited budget who wish to use your talents may offer closer involvement in a project in lieu of fee, or a reduced fee. In these circumstances it is important to weigh up the advantages and disadvantages.

It is important that both you and your client understand the limits of your involvement.

Some things to consider when working with an individual client:

Are the client's expectations of the project realistic?	Can the client demonstrate that the project is achievable?	Will the client's deadline allow you to take on paying projects at the same time?	Will you potentially end up out of pocket if the project goes past its original timescale?

Is it an actual partnership?	Can you be paid at a later date if the project becomes successful?	Can you limit the time the client is allowed to use your imagery to enable fees to be negotiated once the original licence has expired?

YOUR
COMMISSIONERS   PROFESSIONALISM   JOURNALISTIC
                                    AWARENESS

**HOW TO CONTACT
POTENTIAL
CLIENTS**

10

Goodwood Revival
Anna-Louise Felstead 2011

10 Anna-Louise Felstead, location painting, Maserati Birdcage. A number of motor sport paintings grew from a self-initiated project that started at the Monaco Grand Prix Historique. It was a risky venture financially, but Anna-Louise sold enough paintings from the pits to cover costs and was invited to attend another classic car race at Monza. This has resulted in regular race attendance around the world creating artwork for this area: 'Thankfully the work has continued to roll in ever since,' she says, 'so my advice is to take risks!'

WORKING FOR A GLOBAL MARKET: PAUL BUCKLEY, PENGUIN GROUP USA

Paul Buckley is a creative director at Penguin Group USA where he oversees the creation of some of the most interesting book jackets published internationally. Thanks to his father's influence he has been looking at illustration since he was five years old, and consequently is a client who understands how imagery functions and the vocabulary with which artists communicate: 'It's simply something I pay attention to as I'm a massive fan of anyone who draws well – be it comics, tattoo artists or illustrators.' He seems to have a genuine passion for illustration, and that must make him a good client to work with. Paul enthuses, 'Those who do it and make it look effortless, very much impress me.' He recognizes a resurgence of designers and illustrators who do both the design and illustration creating, what he describes as, 'the personally unique covers of today that will be the design icons of tomorrow', when referring enthusiastically to the ranges of covers he worked on with Rachell Sumpter and Matt Taylor:

'I love Rachell's jewel-like palette and it was just a matter of dropping her an email saying: "Hey, can you sew and are you crazy enough to do me three covers flap to flap embroidered?" Luckily Rachell is awesome and game for a cool project. Matt as well – smooth, smooth, smooth, not one hiccup in over ten Le Carre assignments... dreams to work with.'

Being professional is a prerequisite; the design process he describes is rigorous and intense, involving interaction, discussion and negotiation – dealing with aesthetic, technical, commercial concerns. He elucidates: 'When discussing why a designer did this or that, I think what people commenting on book covers seem to gloss over is that the publishers and editors have far more at stake than the cover designer – they have committed sums of money and must answer to the house and the author to make this book a success – so they are very strong about what they think the cover should be, and nothing is being printed without their full consent.'

Paul reveals that he establishes, 'all kinds of relationships as well as non-relationships with illustrators', saying, 'some will become friends, some you'll hear from every couple of years. All's good and what will be will be. I don't need more relationships; I just need to get home before midnight.'

Rachell Sumpter's background was in fine arts – she was intending to study neuroscience but 'was swayed and swooned by art and design'. The delicate paintings for which she is well known, with their sense of enchantment and references to mythology, have been exhibited internationally. Although she says she has, 'focused on print work, books mainly', she adds, 'I am interested in doing just about everything.' The distinctive sense of mark-making and colour appears to be the stylistic connection between her gallery work and the Penguin book jackets, but Rachell identifies the defining aspect of her work as, 'the same thing that defines all artists', adding, 'our fingerprint is in the line work'. That is where her ideas surface. She recognizes there is a distinction within art practice in that, 'anyone can create art, but creating art for the self and creating art with the intent of showing it to others are two different dynamics'. She says she enjoys being her own boss, and of this commission that, 'Paul was a very hands-off art director.'

Networking, and the support of her college peers have been instrumental in gaining work and Rachell describes her college tutors as being incredibly helpful in introducing her to art directors in New York. She reveals that patience is a must when you are an illustrator, admitting that the Penguin commission came several years after she had shown her folio there.

This was a successful and highly regarded commission and the relationship Rachell developed with Paul Buckley as her client is revealed by her reverential description of him: 'Paul is definitely the godfather of cover design – a young godfather.'

1, 2 Cover art for John Le Carré novels published by Penguin USA, by Matt Taylor.

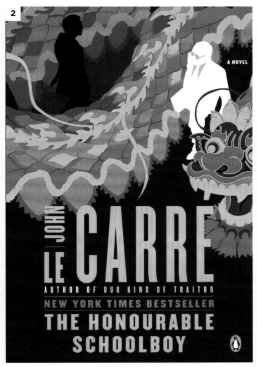

3 Cover art for Penguin USA's *Wind in the Willows*, featuring illustrations by Rachell Sumpter.

WORKING FOR A LOCAL MARKET: GABRIELLE ADAMSON

Gabrielle Adamson has for more than 20 years created a diversity of imagery and hand-drawn lettering that has been used across a myriad of applications.

Gabrielle's business is founded on a system of commendation, which she prefers to actively tout for. She acknowledges, 'I'm easily disheartened by rejection', recognizing that clients come to her because, 'they've seen what I do and like my style.'

Being open to whatever comes along has brought both opportunities and freedom, combined with a degree of financial precariousness – to many of us it would seem unorthodox and alien to barter in lieu of payment, and this type of business requires true enterprise and resilience. Gabrielle recalls, 'I was once paid for a poster for an arts festival with tickets for a classical musical concert. Luckily my landlord was happy to accept the tickets instead of rent.'

In the early stages of Gabrielle's career she was given a batch of granddad shirts in lieu of payment for a sign-writing job. These she batiked and sold on a market stall, which led to a substantial increase in profits. This generated a feature about her work in a national style magazine and the subsequent exposure started a stream of well paid, one-off commissions and she began to create to order. This is an example of self-generated work leading to other commercial avenues – an investment of time and risk-taking resulting in substantial future gain.

Gabrielle has built her career on what she describes as 'word of mouth', combining one-off commissions for local events, businesses and brands with larger commercial clients that bring greater revenue. All generate further exposure but demand constant flexibility.

Gabrielle has sustained her career through being adaptable and versatile, technically and conceptually combining work where she is tightly art directed, which she says, 'sometimes makes me feel like a machine', with jobs that give her more personal freedom, such as hand-painting a coffin, designing fabrics, creating murals and signage for a zoo, and producing her own range of cards and stationery, which she has sold through an arts centre.

The community and location in which Gabrielle works is integral to the narratives and content of her imagery and she is personally connected to much of what she produces, saying, 'It can be disabling to do something unless I know who it's for.' Establishing a reputation and being highly visible has meant that Gabrielle's career is self-perpetuating; she has returning clients and also earns royalties. She has several income streams and there continues to be an authorial dimension to her business alongside more traditional working to commission. In the past few years she has complemented her art business by running an ice cream emporium during the summer where she also sells original artwork and hand-painted objects, revealing pragmatically, 'It's exhausting, but doing artwork can also burn you out, and I like having a break from it.'

Undoubtedly there can be real financial highs and lows in adopting such a parochial approach to business, but the value inherent in becoming truly embedded in the community is difficult to cost.

1 Coffin designed and
hand-painted for an
individual client.
2 Mural painted to commission
for Bradford House, situated
in the area where Gabrielle
Adamson lives and works.

CHAPTER THREE
THE ART OF SELF-PROMOTION

All businesses, whatever products or services they offer, can benefit from advertising to make potential clients or customers aware of their existence. If you are launching yourself as an illustrator, you too should see that promotion is vital to making the market aware of your presence.

Through your choice of promotional materials you will alert potential clients to the type of work that you do and enable them to contact you with work in the future. Some of these potential clients will only be within digital reach, others you may be able to see face-to-face, so you will need various types of promotion appropriate for these differing forms of interaction.

At the early stages of your career, your intention should be to reach the right clients and assert your availability as a professional illustrator. Sending appropriate material to the right people is vital.

Øivind Hovland

HOW DO I GET MYSELF KNOWN?

It is worth taking a holistic approach to your promotion so that whatever stylistic form each separate element may take, there is a visual or conceptual connection within the work.

Many of the products we buy or use every day are identifiable by a logo or by use of particular typefaces, colourways and types of imagery, and by association these elements come to assert the presence, characteristics and qualities of the product. In the same way, the identity you create through your promotional campaign is the packaging to wrap up what you do. In the early stages of your career this branding can reflect the qualities you intend to project about yourself and your work. It also conveys that you are a professional confident about your product.

Just as viral advertising is about building awareness and creating an identity across different but interconnected formats, with strong branding tying them together to enforce an idea, your promotion needs to be planned as a series of separate but tightly associated parts.

When you are commissioned widely and your work is recognizable, the brand is inherent within the work, and this is generally referred to as your 'style'. The identity around your promotion needs to also connect as an extension of what you offer stylistically.

If you consider your promotion as an advertising campaign, it is important to be aware of your audience. Be conscious about the clients you are targeting and how what you offer is either of a higher standard to what others may provide, different to what others offer, or a convenient alternative to what is already available. Being aware of your market is essential – it will lead to you sending relevant promotion to the appropriate potential clients.

1 Paul Davis, promotional badges.

HOW DO I GET
MYSELF KNOWN?

SETTING GOALS

THE DIFFERENT
FORMS OF
PROMOTION

PROMOTING
YOURSELF ONLINE

COMPETITIONS,
EXHIBITIONS AND
TRADE FAIRS

INTERNSHIPS
AND WORK
EXPERIENCE

2

2 Peter Strain,
handwritten self-
promotional packs
containing A6 giclée
prints.

When I graduated I tried to create little projects for myself to help keep my mind focused and try to further develop a style that was beginning to form during my studies. I wanted to target media outlets that had a focus on popular culture so my personal projects included satirical drawings and redesigning film posters.

Once I had gathered the details of who I wanted to contact I put together multiple sets of A6 giclée cards with hand-written notes on why I wanted to work with that specific person/company and a hand-finished wraparound. My hope is that the personal touch combined with the high quality of print/stock will resonate with potential clients and help me stand out.
Peter Strain

PROMOTION – A CLIENT'S PERSPECTIVE: MARTIN COLYER, READER'S DIGEST

Around one in five of the illustrators commissioned by Martin Colyer are the result of the deluge of mailers and promotional materials he receives directly from artists. His inbox testifies to the huge number of emails he receives daily, and he recognizes the investment of time and effort that illustrators make: 'To pay that back one looks through and pins up the things that work for you, and sometimes something really catches your eye and you call and get the illustrator to bring their folio in.'

He advises that hopeful illustrators should research to find the name of the person they are approaching and to, 'focus your efforts on those who'll hire you'. An email or mailer is often the catalyst for the commissioning process and although in itself doesn't provide all the information about the artist, can potentially lead to Martin making the personal connection with the illustrator by inviting them into the office to show their work – something which he clearly values. In contrast to the transience of digital imagery, portfolio visits from selected illustrators can leave a more enduring impression because, 'you get an insight into their working methods, the aspects of certain jobs that they feel didn't quite work, a sense of how they respond to briefs. Insights you can never get from an email or portfolio website.'

Of his favoured form of promotion Martin suggests that, 'in the new media landscape the right craft object might break through'. He describes as examples of this aesthetic; handmade posters, badges and cards and other memorable pieces such as the beautiful tiny origami-like books sent by Roderick Mills, and the wrapping paper from Daniel Frost (pictured opposite): 'I could say that I prefer it to be handed to me by the illustrator after I've looked through their folio, because it sticks in the mind more... Otherwise, something out of the ordinary, or that is memorable or usable as it puts your name or image in front of the commissioner.'

To be memorable is important, and Martin suggests that to make an immediate impression less established illustrators should create a piece of work that 'sums up the best of what you do.' Ultimately, clever promotion cannot compensate for mediocre work and the key to whatever form your promotion takes is what you create as an illustrator: 'Have something that people want to come to you for, be it personality, colour, line, humour, a unique take.'

1, 2 Distinctive promotional
items created by Daniel Frost,
'People and Animals' wrapping
paper and 'Mini Kites' collection.
Martin Colyer reflects on the
impact made by such well
considered artefacts.

SETTING GOALS

You need to adopt a long-term approach to your promotion. Whether you are aiming for longevity in your career, revising your strategy based on the calibre and volume of clients you are getting, or the directions you want to pursue have taken different tangents because your work has evolved, promotion will be pivotal in reaching your objectives. In the early stages of your career, marketing can seem like a thankless task and your response rates may be low or non-existent. It can be easy to lose heart, but perseverance is worthwhile as revising the types of promotion you send out and moulding them to reflect what is new or different about your work could help you to achieve your professional objectives.

Creating appropriate forms of promotion for your work and ensuring that they reach the clients most likely to commission you should be seen as an ongoing and integral dimension of your illustration practice.

Once the app is done you get to the tricky part – getting noticed among the 500,000 plus apps out there. Set up a website for your company and one for your app which clearly demonstrates it. Create an attractive and demonstrative video for the app and set up a PR kit. Last but not least, try to get noticed and talked about on social networks like YouTube, Twitter and Facebook. Unfortunately that is easier said than done, so you need reviews from the countless numbers of game sites and bloggers out there. That is where the video and PR kit comes in. If you are lucky to get reviewed you can enhance the impact by running web banners on these sites. If you don't, run banners anyway.
Problem Bob

3 Homepage of Problem Bob's website, detailing their apps and other sites.
4 Evgenia Barinova, promotional New Year's card.

HOW DO I GET
MYSELF KNOWN?

SETTING GOALS

THE DIFFERENT
FORMS OF
PROMOTION

PROMOTING
YOURSELF ONLINE

COMPETITIONS,
EXHIBITIONS AND
TRADE FAIRS

INTERNSHIPS
AND WORK
EXPERIENCE

Levels of promotion

Apart from financial constraints which will influence the forms your promotion will take, there are practical considerations to be aware of:

— Promotion must be representative of your work; the images you choose should reflect what you do – stylistically and conceptually. The image on a card that you leave a client should also connect visually to your website or digital folio.

— Your promotion should be functional – can it be accessed quickly and efficiently by your potential client? Can you send it easily through the post? Do images open quickly if digital? Are your contact details easily accessible? Is it memorable?

— If your name and contact details are on the front of any promotion you send, check they won't be hidden if your image is displayed face forward on a wall or desk.

— Luck can play a part in when and where to send out your promotion – the image on a card may be just what the client was looking for on the day that it was received. Generally though, there are cycles in commissioning processes. Large publishing houses' annual schedules are dictated by the dates of major book fairs and seasonal launches. Magazines often have specific days for commissioning but will be too busy to take calls on press day. The stationery and greetings industry is cyclical. The major calendar events which shape life can also influence industry. Making contact with the appropriate person during summer holidays and festive periods may be more difficult. You need to become aware of the invisible industry calendar and know when to make optimum impact with the promotion you choose to send.

— Thousands of graduates will emerge from art colleges annually, hoping to begin their own businesses. You need to be seen in the forums where early career professionals launch their practices but shouldn't rely solely on them as the launch pad for your career, or see them as the only mechanism for your promotion.

I believe that the best promotion is to keep creating good work both personally and commercially. This approach hasn't changed since I started my career. It sounds quite simplistic but I believe that it is important to not compromise, and to do the best to my ability for each piece of work that I create.
Natsko Seki

5 Natsko Seki, illustration from 'Autumn', a passport-shaped mini catalogue for Louis Vuitton, Japan.

PROMOTION – A CLIENT'S PERSPECTIVE: CHOI LIU, HEAD OF ART BUYING AT M&C SAATCHI

Choi Liu is a rare client because she loves illustration, understands the art and craft of image-making and sees that it is part of her job to make time to see who is out there. She says enthusiastically, 'I have to source the right illustrator for the job. I think it's the most interesting role in advertising.' She is passionate about keeping her finger on the pulse, looking at everything.

She opens all her own mail, personally going through all the samples which she receives, revealing, 'I keep the most interesting stuff, but throw a lot away. Illustrators should do their research to find out what the clients they approach are doing; otherwise it's a waste of time on their front and a waste of money.'

The most popular forms of promotion are postcards and email updates and she has received various sized posters, booklets and cotton bags with illustrations printed on. She appreciates whatever is out of the norm, a couple of favourites being a handmade 3D ice lolly and a house-shaped Christmas decoration (pictured opposite), both made from paper and card by Hattie Newman.

Every day at 11am and 4pm she makes time to look at portfolios, occasionally asking the illustrator to call in because she is keen to, 'understand their personality as well as their style.' She is drawn to individuals rather than agents, saying, 'I prefer the smaller agencies, some agencies are so vast I wouldn't want to be in a stable like that if I were an illustrator.' The personal connection she makes is important, 'I always remember people I meet. If you're passionate about your images it comes through. If you can put that across in front of a client hopefully they will also be enthusiastic.'

Perhaps it is her own experience as a craft-based designer and a love of art developed during childhood that fuels her continued appreciation and her enthusiasm for interesting examples of original artwork: 'Some agents show me work on iPads, but I'd rather see a folio with one or two well-chosen originals.' Sadly, she says she is often disappointed with what is available, reflecting, 'It's hardly ever that I come across anyone with any originality, someone with craft or someone who draws brilliantly.' Although when she comes across someone who's amazing, 'it's like a breath of fresh air, I run around the agency showing everyone!'

Advertising is big business and whilst she points out that, 'illustration on a billboard will make you stop immediately and look at it', she believes that choosing the right people is important and that illustration is not suitable for every campaign. She clarifies on this point: 'Some illustrators are not so commissionable for the type of work we do. You want them to do well because they are so talented, but it may not be every day that someone with a very specific style will get work.' She is critical of illustrators who are pale imitations of a current trend or stylistic fad: 'I think for longevity illustrators need an original style.'

Choi is not fazed by illustrators' geographic locations, language differences, nor if they are inexperienced, and she scouts for new talent at the major graduate shows, but says standards are not always what she would hope for: 'It's frightening to think there are so many illustrators out there, and so many who are not prepared. It's tough; it's really hard to make a living. So many illustrators just out of college don't have a sense of direction; they need to know who to take their work to.'

1 Advertising for ITV, illustrated by Marc Burckhardt, commissioned by M&C Saatchi, selected by Choi Liu.
2 Innovative promotional materials in the form of Christmas decorations by illustrator Hattie Newman.
3 Billboard advertising as part of a campaign by Transport for London. Illustrated by Serge Bloch, commissioned by M&C Saatchi, selected by Choi Liu.

For Christmas and New Year travel information visit tfl.gov.uk or pick up a leaflet at Tube stations

MAYOR OF LONDON

Transport for London

THE DIFFERENT FORMS OF PROMOTION

There are many forms of promotion – their function can be evaluated in terms of your own business objectives at any time.

Essential – a digital presence, an email account and a phone number combined with an additional form of direct mail, either hard copy or digital.

Highly desirable – presence in source books, limited edition promotional pieces or promotional events. A marketing or PR assistant.

Desirable – paid folio sites, other printed mail-outs.

You will need a strategy for the promotion and marketing of your work. You are aiming to reach a substantial number of clients over a long time period, and you will approach this in different ways depending upon the particular stage of your career. You may decide to pay a substantial amount of money for a page in a source book to launch your career, or to spend time putting together a blog and sending out cards for a fraction of the cost. Both examples are viable options – it depends on the type of work you do and what is the best mechanism to reach your audience. A lavish piece of promotion will never convince a magazine that has no budget for illustration that they should commission you. If you have a blog and create an email mailer that is sent to the right potential clients your first pieces of promotion will be effectively inexpensive. After this there will inevitably be costs involved with whatever additional forms of promotion you plan to use, but the extent of this needs to be considered and how you manage these costs reflected in your overall business plan.

What kind of promotion do I need?

There are many forms of promotion, some of which are given below, although this is not an exclusive list:

— business cards

— logos

— letterheads

— rubber stamps

— stickers

— postcards

— artefacts

— small books

— image packs

— posters

— digital files

— websites

— portfolios

— portfolio websites

— dummy books

— online folios

— showreels

— juried annuals

— source books

— exhibitions

— novelty items

— ads in trade papers

— press releases

— stalls in a market

— stands at trade events

It is important to consider which areas of the market you are hoping to get work from and what is suitable in terms of the content of imagery and nature of the promotional piece. Where possible, do as much research as you can to find out what is acceptable – for example, many large publishing houses will publish submissions guidelines either on their websites or in publications such as the *Writers' & Artists' Yearbook* (A&C Black).

I'm such a small enterprise that it doesn't take much to coordinate a small promotional campaign. My hope is that by producing work with a consistent spirit and energy over a long time, I'm able to develop a brand of sorts, but I don't have brand statements and big billboard campaigns for myself! My approach is to send the same thing to a number of people, but hand-make them and include a personalized note. I want to make the package exciting for its recipient to open, and also fun for me to make. I'll do about two or three promotional send-outs a year – normally at Christmas and in the summer, and then if I've got a new website or upcoming exhibition. I usually make my promotional gifts out of materials I already have and I set myself a budget for postage. I'm more aware of the time it takes me to make all the identical gifts... I've never made more than 30 at one time, but it's always time consuming and I often underestimate how long it will take!
Hattie Newman

HOW DO I GET
MYSELF KNOWN?   SETTING GOALS   **THE DIFFERENT
FORMS OF
PROMOTION**   PROMOTING
YOURSELF ONLINE   COMPETITIONS,
EXHIBITIONS AND
TRADE FAIRS   INTERNSHIPS
AND WORK
EXPERIENCE

6

6 Pomme Chan, a series of
promotional pieces sent out
to new and existing clients.
Photograph by Oat-Chaiyasith.

**Each year I do different promo. I
like doing different things as I get
bored easily and it's so much fun
to see my works not only on screen
or paper but also on products.
It gives clients a better idea of
how my illustration can go live.**
Pomme Chan

PROMOTION AS PART OF PRACTICE: JACK TEAGLE

'Big projects can get a lot of visibility, and clients get in touch with me because they liked previous projects that I worked on,' says Jack Teagle, an illustrator who optimizes the many platforms available whilst recognizing that ultimately it is his work that probably serves as the best form of promotion. He rarely contacts potential clients directly, relying instead on the impact created when new work is released and the exposure gained through the wide distribution of these pieces internationally. He refers in particular to his comic books published by Nobrow Press, describing them as 'calling cards', which reveal his versatility of approach: 'They've helped to spread my name in America and I've been able to work with some great American clients as a result of them being passed around offices and workplaces.'

Jack also emphasizes the value of the Web as a mechanism for generating interest, stressing the importance of his blog, which he constantly updates, for reaching a broad audience and attracting potential clients in the same way as viral advertising does: 'Fans will re-post images, share things, write about my work and it spreads like wildfire.'

He benefits from a word-of-mouth culture, with the enthusiasm for what he posts often translating into further commissions: 'I have a bit of an online following, and I know that a few art directors and people working within the industry watch for what I'm doing, so that works out. It brings in jobs.'

Jack sees it is important to complement this broad and more serendipitous exposure with considered targeting of art editors. He focuses on avenues where his visual approach will be appropriate, mostly using mail-outs. This more strategic process, being selective about who to approach with what work, has evolved through experience: 'It was much more desperate when I graduated! I used to send cards to any art director's address that I could get my hands on. It's better to think things through, and send fewer emails. That saves a lot of time and you don't have to deal with so many rejections!'

Jack recognizes that alongside his own promotional activities, agent representation with YCN, 'gives me a professional platform.' He acknowledges that this endorses the commercial viability of the more esoteric and authorial dimensions of his practice, adding, 'I think when some clients see that I work through an agent it almost acts as a seal of approval, like it gives a legitimate feel.'

Promotion is more than a bolt-on marketing activity – it is intrinsic to Jack's practice, ingrained within him: 'Even when I was little I would tirelessly self-promote my own little comics and try to sell them in school... it's a great way to make new contacts and friends too.'

1 'Cats and Pumpkins', A3 risograph print.
2 *The Jungle*, comic for McSweeny's.
3 Wrestling figures created for ELCAF (East London Comics and Arts Festival).

PROMOTING YOURSELF ONLINE

Website

Blogs

There is no question that an online presence is required to let the world know you are ready to be commissioned. Your artwork will be ready for viewing from across the globe, encouraging the possibility of receiving international attention. A commercial artist who cannot be accessed through the Web is severely limiting their opportunities to present their wares to the broadest possible commissioner base.

There are many ways to promote your artwork online, from a personal website or blog through to commercial portfolio websites and social networking sites. A combination of these will further increase your visibility.

A personal website acts as an online portfolio displaying your work. You will have to pay for a domain name and hosting of the site, which is usually available for varying time periods. Select a relevant name for your site and contact email address – it will be around for a long time, and something frivolous may not be appropriate once you are more established. Website packages are available, or you can commission a web designer or build your own if you have the skills. Images can be ordered into various sections according to your requirements (portfolio, new work, personal work). The site homepage needs to clearly signpost where your images are, your contact details, a link to your blog if you have one and commissioned imagery.

To keep clients coming back, it is important to keep your site updated – even if you have a blog to support it. If the last image uploaded is from a year ago it can look stale and imply that you are not effectively organized, thus discouraging repeat viewing. Clear contact information is also imperative, and ensure that the email address is one that you regularly log into. Missing an enquiry could lose you a commission.

The effectiveness of a website relies on its clarity, ease of navigation, and speed of loading. If viewers have to watch the counter rise to 100 every time they access an image, their patience may expire before they have had the chance to see more than a small selection. Remember that online image files should only be at 72 dpi and saved for web, ensuring that they appear instantly and cannot be easily appropriated for unauthorized print use.

Blogs are a type of website that contain images and type with generally the most recent item or post displayed first, giving them a very current feel – assuming they are regularly updated, which is recommended. The styles of blogs range from the simple to the increasingly sophisticated, emulating the layout of a website. The advantages are ease of access to update artwork and text, and the perception that they are less formal than websites, giving more intimate access to the artist's world. It is important to recognize that blog content aimed at potential commissioners should not be mixed in the same blog with very personal information. You may wish to embrace the informality of a blog, but images from a hilarious night out with friends do not sit well with presentation of new work or enhance the professionalism of your attitude. Official 'followers' of your blog should be encouraged, as higher numbers will help boost your blog in search results.

Word-of-mouth will get your site noticed, but as that is not guaranteed, it is essential that you regularly inform prospective clients that your site is up there waiting for their attention, and focus your promotion to drive attention to your site. Tracking hits to your site after a mail-out or email campaign will give you a tangible assessment of its effectiveness. Statistics can be accessed through your hosting site. Linking with other sites and having a presence on forums and discussions will also bring traffic to your site or blog.

HOW DO I GET
MYSELF KNOWN?   SETTING GOALS   THE DIFFERENT
FORMS OF
PROMOTION   **PROMOTING
YOURSELF
ONLINE**   COMPETITIONS,
EXHIBITIONS AND
TRADE FAIRS   INTERNSHIPS
AND WORK
EXPERIENCE

7
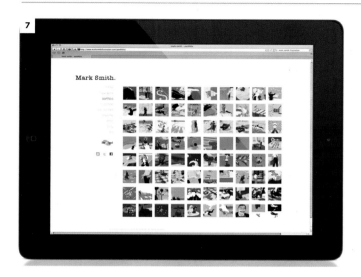

8
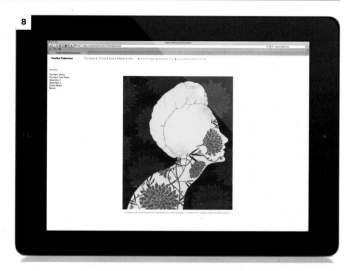

9

10

7 Mark Smith's website: www.marksmithillustration.com
8 Yvetta Fedorova's website: www.scottmenchin.com
9 Holly Exley's website: www.hollyexley.blogspot.co.uk
10 Zachariah OHora's website: www.zachohorastudio.blogspot.co.uk

Portfolio websites

Portfolio websites are commercial enterprises set up to showcase a substantial number of artists' work, charging an annual fee for an individual space as part of an aggregation of folios. They do not have the personal element of an individual site, and you are side by side with your competition – but they do have the positive benefit of increased traffic from potential commissioners drawn by a large number of images and styles on offer, and can present you to a new global audience. Promotion of the site will be through e-newsletters and online and print adverts, often with featured artists displayed.

Management of the individual portfolios within the site should be easy for the artists to access and use, with the option to tag your images with relevant words to facilitate client searches. Search options should be effective to aid easy access to images grouped under subject matter, style or genre of work and names of artists.

Social networking

Social networking websites continue to play an increasingly large part in networking and self-promotion for freelance creatives, although social and professional networking sites operate differently. Professional sites such as LinkedIn allow users to connect with other professionals and build up a network of people who can be updated on work and activities; these tend to be more formal than sites which encourage display of artwork, comment and interaction.

Social sites have a more informal approach, but can still be used to show work. They all have a different feel so it is worth assessing what is out there and selecting which you feel comfortable with. Some sites, such as the content-based Behance, focus on a more professional interface, but any that allow images to be posted could result in exposure to art directors, and updating your network on new work and commissions can be an unforced way of promotion. Also, take note of how images can be tagged within the site which may impact on general searches being done by commissioners and increase the likelihood of being found. Add links to your social media from your website or blog.

As with blogs, consider the mix of the personal and the professional, and check privacy settings and the terms and conditions of sites to ensure that any rights to your images do not transfer to the website.

Social media word-of-mouth is developing as an avenue for promotion through micro-blogging with Twitter, and creators can find it also works as a beneficial social tool and source of people who provide inspiration and feedback. Time needs to be invested in this form of promotion to build a profile and it will require constant attention to build up a following. The larger your following, the more likely you are to be noticed, so sharing relevant and interesting information with your network may attract clients.

It is a natural inclination to want to display your latest creation online, and this is fine for self-generated imagery. But it is important that any commissioned work is not exposed prior to it being published by the client, unless you have specific permission from them to do so. Most commissioners will ask that work you produce for them is exclusive to them, meaning only they can reproduce it for the length of the licence you have granted them; it could also compromise their product if it is revealed before the launch date.

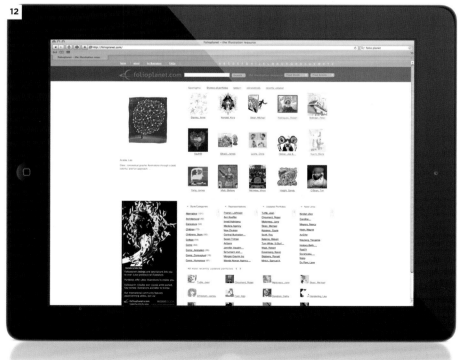

I think people are interested in following individuals, so illustrators on social media have the capacity to become hugely popular. Presenting yourself in an informal, honest manner can earn you a large following, meaning your work has wider visibility online, and having a few specific angles means that you'll be remembered for your talents. I've been put forward for a few jobs through my following online, so it's worth stressing where your niche is. I also see a lot of art directors and magazine editors presenting themselves in an informal manner through Twitter for example, so perhaps it's easier to make a connection with them personally, as opposed to sending faceless emails.
Holly Exley

11 Homepage for the ispot, an online hub for illustrators, where they can market their own work: www.theispot.com.
12 Homepage for Folio Planet, an online directory of illustrators and their portfolios: www.folioplanet.com.

COMPETITIONS, EXHIBITIONS AND TRADE FAIRS

As well as targeting specific art directors as potential clients for work, you can generate interest in what you do and reach a potentially broader audience by entering competitions. They are international and respected phenomena, often providing for you as an illustrator the incentive to create new work and to answer briefs which may challenge your work in new ways. Apart from the tangible rewards coming from being selected as an award winner – ranging from monetary prizes, trips, book deals, publication in prestigious annuals and exhibitions, being printed in high-profile design formats – there is the sense of personal achievement gained from having entered. If you are successful, this is a solid endorsement of the quality of what you create and a signal to potential clients that your excellence has been recognized. There are several other pros and cons of entering competitions:

Pros

• Your work is often seen by respected industry specialists.

• Competitions generate publicity so there are often opportunities for further exposure.

• Clients often check out awards as part of their illustration research.

• The annuals and magazines associated with some of the more established competitions have a long shelf life and are distributed widely throughout the industry.

• Awards are a good excuse to remind clients that you exist and to make a big publicity splash.

• An award can be added to your CV or resumé.

Cons

• Some of the prizes lead to publication deals which may involve you handing over your rights or demand subsequent exclusivity in the artwork.

• Some competitions can lead to you paying excessively for printing or other associated costs.

• There is the possibility that your entry automatically becomes the intellectual property of the competition host.

There is a very thin line between my commercial work and exhibition work. I see my exhibition work as the play garden in which there are no rules whatsoever. As a trained illustrator I make my basic income with illustration and that gives me the space to experiment in my personal work. Selling isn't the main motivation. However, very often people from the creative industry see more personal work in a gallery or on the Web and see possibilities to use it commercially. When the right client comes along this provides an opportunity to work on commercial projects that are very close to your heart. This is also the reason I decided to mix both commercial and personal work on my website and not make two separate portfolios. There is also a downside to this: art directors are sometimes afraid to work with me because they think it's too 'arty' whilst curators often think it's not art but design.

Merijn Hos

HOW DO I GET
MYSELF KNOWN?   SETTING GOALS   THE DIFFERENT
FORMS OF
PROMOTION   PROMOTING
YOURSELF ONLINE   **COMPETITIONS,
EXHIBITIONS AND
TRADE FAIRS**   INTERNSHIPS
AND WORK
EXPERIENCE

13 Merijn Hos, self-initiated
exhibition work: wooden
sculptures for an exhibition at
Stedelijk Museum Kampen.

14 Merijn Hos, commercial
work: a typographic piece for
the Fader x (RED) campaign.

Exhibitions as part of the campaign

Many competitions culminate in exhibitions of artwork. Whether in a show of this nature, a curated group exhibition which you have contributed to as an individual artist, or a one-person exhibition, having your work seen 'off the page' in public spaces can be a valuable form of exposure. The location and nature of the venue is important to the potential value of any exhibition. Ideally the content should reflect the audience you hope to reach through commissions, although shows provide the opportunity to explore new avenues for your work and potentially reach a divergent audience. Unexpected trade can be gained from showing work in busy locations where there is a broad demographic.

Before embarking upon involvement in any exhibition, gauge the potential impact it will have and the opportunities it may bring. The status of venue isn't necessarily important if you can get the right people interested in seeing it and blogging about it afterwards.

Below are some factors to be aware of when embarking upon an exhibition:

• Imagery commissioned or created for a specific illustrative purpose can sometimes lose some of its value and meaning when removed from its applied context and sited in an unconnected exhibition setting.

• Preparing an exhibition can be demanding of resources – the actual costs of mounting, marketing, signage and launch, as well as time in preparation, hanging and transportation, need to be considered.

• If you are in a joint show you can gain or lose status by association – check the nature and quality of other exhibitors.

• A solo show can be a big commitment. Build the preparation, marketing and staging of this into your wider work and business plan.

• Exhibitions are a speculative activity; there is no guarantee that any outlay will bring immediate or longer-term commercial returns.

Trade fairs

Trade fairs are a more formal type of exhibition. These can range from large corporate events dealing with the high end of business around illustration, such as the Bologna Children's Book Fair where rights are negotiated between publishers of children's books internationally, character licensing fairs where large media and publishing deals are struck, to smaller scale comic book conventions or print fairs. Generally, trade fairs focus on a particular dimension of the market and present the opportunity to encounter a density of related practitioners and potential clients. Attendance at trade fairs is an efficient way to undertake research of concentrated areas of the market. If you have appropriate stock or products, participation at a fair can be an expedient way of directly reaching your potential market.

15 SURTEX, trade show for selling and licensing original art and design. Images courtesy of Penny Sikalis, vice president of GLM shows.

I was fortunate enough to be selected for the AOI Images 'Best of British Illustration' exhibition and tour that brought my work to the attention of M&C Saatchi a month before my first solo show. Being a part of these events was a massive promotional boost which helped get my work in front of a lot of people I may have found difficult to do otherwise, and resulted in my solo show being extended for two months.

Stuart Whitton

16 Stuart Whitton, 'The Devil is in the Details' typographic illustration created for Stuart's own solo exhibition 'Origins'.

INTERNSHIPS AND WORK EXPERIENCE

An understanding of the industry you are hoping to enter can be very beneficial, and work experience or an internship can offer a chance to experience first-hand facets of the business that you would be unlikely to access as an independent freelancer. Some of these positions may offer a wage, others will be purely voluntary paying only travel expenses. It is important that you recognize which type of work you are being offered and if what you may be asked to do for the organization is appropriate. You should not be standing at the photocopier all day. The experience should be relevant for your CV or resumé, and hopefully a rewarding one.

Assisting within an organization means you are there to learn about what they do, how it is done, and to learn or expand on new skills. As such, there will be an expectation that you will want to ask questions. Make the most of this and try and focus what you are asking. Concentrate on what it is you want to know. Rather than asking: 'How do I get commissions?' enquire about the best forms of self-promotion they have seen, or who they believe is currently commissioning the most interesting illustration work, and use the responses to build a broad understanding. Pick the right time for asking questions; asking one of the team to set aside some time with you over a coffee, maybe outside the often busy office environment, will mean that you have their full attention and will stop you from feeling that you might be interrupting their schedule.

The business side of the industry is often overlooked in college and internships can enhance your understanding of this area. Experience in an office environment may allow you to gain transferrable skills, which will be positive for many areas of future employment and will give you an understanding of some of the pressures your future commissioners may be under in their roles.

When applying for an internship or work experience it is important to make a positive impression right from the start. You will generally be asked to supply a CV or resumé when applying, and how this looks and reads is important. Avoid the temptation to decorate it with images, keeping information clear and concise. Include all work experience, even if it is that call centre job you did for two months and couldn't wait to leave – it may be considered a useful skill if you are asked to do research.

If it is a position where your artistic skills may be required, attach some samples in a low-resolution PDF with your application. However, be aware that if you would be working in a more administrative capacity, it could appear that you have not read the description of the role properly, expecting instead a more creative position.

It is likely that you will be given an interview prior to being offered a position, and it is a good idea to take this opportunity to ask questions about the expectations of the organization as well as demonstrating that you have done some homework on what they do. Being friendly and presentable will help make a good impression.

17

Working as an agent was really insightful. I got a much better idea of pricing and the pitfalls to watch out for when working for different types of clients such as reading the small print when signing over rights to your work. Also, just seeing the various styles of work that get commissioned was quite a learning curve – for example, which work is the most commercial.
Kate Evans

17 Kate Evans, 'India', self-promotional piece. Kate is represented by Folio, having worked as an agent herself previously.

USING A VARIED PROMOTIONAL STRATEGY: MARK SMITH

A strong sense of idea and narrative is evident in Mark Smith's work, and the success he now enjoys comes from establishing a reputation as an illustrator who consistently comes up with concepts delivered in his fresh and distinctive visual language. He considers the part that promotion made in launching his career: 'This sounds so shallow but I love competitions, they were probably my first form of promotion. Some of the student competitions gave me the confidence to follow up on what I was doing with my work, and provided me with some momentum to carry into the industry after graduation.'

He has benefitted personally from the motivating dimension of having work selected, enjoying the honour that this bestowed, as well as professionally gaining from the exposure: 'As all of the images have been through some kind of quality control the promotional potential is great. I think some competition success can help buyers make a quality evaluation about a person's work. I don't mean to suggest that a career should be shaped around the results of competitions, but the recognition seems to be an important part of an overall marketing strategy.'

He has a clear idea of the inter-connecting functions of the varying forms of digital presence he now undertakes, saying, 'I see my own portfolio (and url) as the showcase, the blog offers a bit of background info about me and my work, and the paid portfolio sites, such as theispot and altpick, show that I'm taking the work seriously enough to invest in the promotion of it alongside other professionals.' He sees part of the decision to be visible on paid sites as contributing to asserting his brand: 'I don't think relying on a free blog, or the free portfolio sites, is enough to show that you're serious about what you're doing.' In the early stages of his career he combined digital promotion with mailing lists to ensure that the right people were made aware of his presence: 'Initially I augmented the Association of Illustrators client lists with my own research,' he laughs, 'I was thrown out of a big newsagent's once for leafing through their magazines looking for contacts, I'd been in there for around an hour and a half so I guess it was to be expected!' He says that although he doesn't ask where clients came across his work he thinks that because of the direct access to potential clients, mailing lists have been good value for money. He reflects, 'If you get busy after a mailshot then it's done a good job. The portfolio sites do a slightly different job for me, and I think they're a bit more of a slow burner, but necessary all the same.'

Although not consciously evaluating the success and evolving function of his promotion, Mark recognizes that it serves a different purpose for him now that he is established and has agents successfully representing him in the UK and USA: 'Initially I was using promotion to show people that I exist and to try to get a flow of work coming in. Now that I've got a volume of work out there, rather than shouting about my existence it feels more like I'm showing different aspects of my character.'

Promotion remains integral to Mark's career: 'I've tried to spend every waking minute developing and understanding my work itself, where I want to take it, what I want to do with it and what I want to get out of it. I think an interesting/quirky marketing campaign would be fantastic but at the moment I'm still more focused on the actual work: my promotion offers a window into that.'

1 Illustration for the article 'How to Manage Staff that Fail Under Pressure', *Public Finance* magazine.
2 Illustration depicting 'Modern living habits', for *The New York Times*.
3 Book cover illustration for *Collected Stories of Rumpole*, published by Penguin.
4 'Bullied Schoolgirl', for *You Magazine*.

HOW WORK EXPERIENCE CAN HELP YOUR CAREER: LIBBY MCMULLIN

As an undergraduate student, Libby had work experience entailing several weeks working in-house for a major greetings card publisher. Although operating in this area had not been an overt ambition, she acknowledges, 'The industry warmed to me and accepted my style.'

Shortly after graduating, Tigerprint (a division of Hallmark Cards) commissioned her to design for UK high-street store Marks & Spencer and the brief expanded what she had learned as an intern, setting the direction for her career: 'Although I was still at an experimental stage,' she recalls, 'they took me under their wing, and I watched my illustrations come to life on giftware products and stationery.'

Reflecting that every subsequent opportunity within the design industry, 'through trials and hardships as well as great achievement has been an experience to help me grow', she reveals that the early work experience was pivotal to the direction of her business, and that equally, 'each company I have designed for since has fuelled my desire to be succssful.' This now includes major international companies of cards and giftware.

Libby views the greeting card industry as a platform for promotion and for exploring future opportunities, and she now runs her own greeting card publishing company online and in boutiques. In addition, she sells directly through a market stall at Camden Lock, London. This she describes as, 'an open portfolio for the world to see,' using it as a medium to test out new designs on the general public, emphasizing: 'I don't need to rely on knowing when my next freelance work will come in now, and the direct contact with the customers has given me a huge amount of confidence and a sense of enterprise and motivation that I feel was lacking before.'

Although Libby doesn't send out promotional material, the combination of this exposure with presence at international trade shows such as Progressive Greetings Live, Top Drawer, SURTEX and Brand Licensing Europe maximizes the opportunity to reach the broadest audience: 'I keep my eyes open for opportunities everywhere I go', she says. 'I tell budding illustrators to enter competitions because even if they are not chosen as a winner, their work is seen.' With sites such as Twitter, Facebook and Instagram, she believes, 'A designer must do it all if they want a following and fan base.' She advocates a proactive approach to building a business, suggesting enthusiastically, 'an illustration shouldn't sit in your portfolio under your bed, waiting for someone to ask to see it.'

Gaining a solid, in-depth understanding of this area of the illustration industry has provided a firm base from which Libby has built her career and the confidence to be in control. She sees it as more than her business, stating: 'the passion I have for my work is what makes me an accepted industry professional.'

1 'If You Jump, You Might Fly', greetings card design.
2 'Powder Puff Girl', a fashion illustration commissioned for a charity event.
3 Bespoke illustration for a wedding.
4 'Alice', a fashion illustration for a private commission.

SELF-PROMOTION – AN AGENT'S PERSPECTIVE: LOUISA ST PIERRE – BERNSTEIN & ANDRIULLI

Bernstein & Andriulli is an internationally known management agency representing a wide stable of illustrators, photographers, stylists and producers. They are based in New York and have affiliations with agencies in Europe and an office in Shanghai. Having a broad client list, including many of the largest corporations, publications and associations globally, means that to be represented by them provides an artist with the potential to work within the most prestigious and lucrative areas of illustration.

As well as actively scouting for talent by visiting graduate shows and generally having heightened awareness of the work being commissioned, the agency are approached directly on a constant basis by illustrators hoping for representation. Louisa St Pierre reveals that a combination of important skills and expertise needs to be evident, but also that their choice can be influenced by trends. She clarifies by giving a current example: 'Vector character development is in huge demand right now, for print and motion branding, entertainment, packaging and of course interactive needs like augmented reality, apps and game development.' In this situation, the agent is looking for specific talents. Practitioners demonstrating exemplary aptitude in doing these kinds of work will be more likely to register on the radar.

When describing what the agency is looking for in a promotional piece, Louisa says, 'I guess marketability is an accurate but ambiguous answer.' They receive pieces of promotion fitting all descriptions; some lavishly produced artefacts, as well as more simple mailers.

Louisa stresses the importance of presentation in all pieces; the need to pay attention to the craft and design aspects, as well as their functionality in terms of leading to and showcasing the illustrator's work: 'Shotopop, for example, sent a wonderful hardback book of their latest and greatest work, with a die-cut, monochromatic, slip cover, when they were seeking representation. Every beautifully laid out page was a treat, encouraging one to check out their website advertised in the book, which of course was also outstanding in design and content, not to mention easy to navigate. We met with them immediately and signed them.'

In the digital age where everything is readily available on screen, work can often seem ephemeral. The agency enjoys receiving individual and potentially more memorable items. Louisa advises, 'It's worth noting that it is essential that the marketing materials to which your promo leads (and your follow-up email to the lucky recipient) are equal in excellence. Your branding must be consistent.'

For an artist planning to invest in a special form of promotion for a more memorable approach to an agent, she suggests some of the types of artefacts that may be worth considering: 'Something utilitarian like a good old calendar, notepad, phone app or bag that folks can integrate into their everyday lives is practical, helpful and a constant reminder of your work.'

The idea can be an enduring reminder of an artist. If being clever or witty or thought-provoking is your forté, it can be a vital aspect of any promotional campaign and needn't put the costs up. Louisa endorses this point, 'An item articulating a little jokette can be fun too, if you want to articulate the humour in your work. Karlssonwilker created a pencil that said "This is your Dad's computer on the side". Ha!'

1, 2, 3, 4 Shotopop's *Black Blossoms: A Collection of Curiosities*, a promotional hardcover book. Shotopop are represented by Bernstein & Andriulli.

CHAPTER FOUR
GETTING YOUR
WORK SEEN

Your website, physical portfolio and digital communications are platforms for you to demonstrate your capabilities to potential clients. In business terms these are key tools for selling your product and they complement each other in their functions.

The presentation of your work to an art director needs to be an efficient and informative process, and you need to make an impact and leave a clear and lasting impression. Clients are likely to have limited time and the work of many other artists available to them, so you need to be compelling and memorable.

Structuring your site around a hierarchy with clear categories to facilitate easy navigation will make it easy for potential clients to dip into your website's content, selecting sections relevant to their needs. Looking at other sites and understanding how other illustrators have done this will help you to decide the appropriate groupings of your own work and help you to organize your images accordingly. Categories may relate to areas you have worked in, showcase your favourite images or simply separate commissions from personal work.

Kanitta Meechubot

ORGANIZING YOUR FOLIO AND WEBSITE

It is likely that your folio will be looked at in sequence from beginning to end. For this reason you need to customize the content based on the specific needs of each possible client – making considered selections from your larger body of work. The physicality of your work, such as textural qualities of an original piece of artwork, can introduce a wow factor that is more difficult to achieve on screen. There are fundamental issues underpinning the creation of both folio and website.

Be relevant

Choose artwork that reflects the areas of work you aspire to. You are making a series of statements about yourself, your skills and your suitability to be commissioned. Be conscious of the projected needs of specific clients and try to see what you present from their external perspective. Your college life drawings are unlikely to be relevant in a commercial portfolio unless you are pitching for a job requiring similar kinds of imagery. On your website, however, a drawing section may offer another dimension of your practice without diluting the impact of your commercial work.

Be selective

You can make an impression in your portfolio with a relatively small number of images if you choose the right pieces of work. Often your university folio will have been arranged chronologically and contain everything you submitted for assessments. Your professional folio has different objectives, and it makes sense to group images according to their function and content irrespective of when or for what purpose they were originally created. There is no definitive guide to achieving this – if a group of artwork shows an idea evolving with visual consistency over a range of applications, it may be appropriate to keep it together. If you were experimental across the project and the work includes variable outcomes in terms of visual approach and quality you may want to choose the pieces which best represent the direction you aspire towards. Consistency and cohesion are key to making a memorable impact.

1 A spread from Robin Heighway-Bury's portfolio.

ORGANIZING
YOUR FOLIO
AND WEBSITE

VISUAL LITERACY

AGENT
REPRESENTATION

Demonstrate
commercial potential

You may need to produce mock-ups showing work in appropriate commercial contexts, or art direct yourself to produce additional samples – demonstrating that you can a handle a brief. The application of more esoteric work in well-designed mock-ups integrated within your folio can suggest potential applications to future clients.

If you have limited typographical and design skills, it's best to find an aesthetically appropriate pre-existing design context to apply your images to rather than creating the entire context yourself. Taking a magazine layout, book jacket or packaging design are good starting points.

If you are sufficiently competent to handle the entire mock-up, what you produce may also create possible opportunities across design, so it pays to be clear in your captions as to what you have produced.

My website conveys the message that my illustrations work sequentially to show changing thoughts and feelings. The 'projects' page and link to my blog show my work in progress and the processes behind my work.
Lesley White

2 Lesley White's website, showing illustrations for *The House Rabbit*, published by David Fickling books: www.lesleywhite.co.uk

2

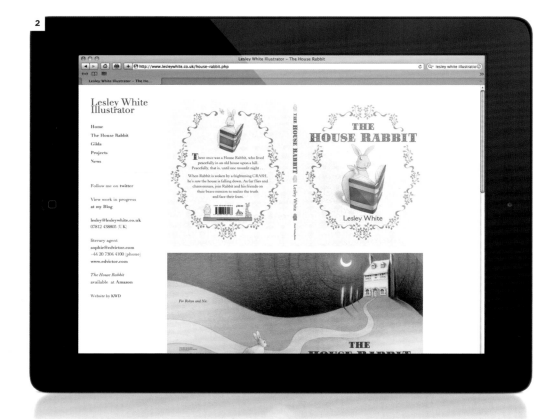

VISUAL LITERACY

Illustrators operate in environments where there is often a high degree of visual literacy. The organization, layout and navigation through your folio and website should therefore be considered as a design exercise. Your folio is often referred to as your 'book' and considering the pace and sequence of the folio is important. Consider how each spread opens within the context of the whole folio and how you strategically create maximum impact by the positioning of each one.

In both your website and folio, decisions made on typefaces, colour schemes, editing and layout of content will make a design statement. This should connect to the choices you have made for other pieces of promotion, such as your letterheads, business cards and mailers. You are establishing a brand identity.

Be aware of reproduction qualities. Poor printouts won't do your work justice and may suggest that you don't pay attention to the details.

Process and methodology

Some clients like to see back-up work, such as character development or a range of concepts leading to a finished idea. The placing of these elements of your process needs to be integral to the design of your entire folio. Lumpy sketchbooks which also contain shopping lists should be avoided, although selected pages could be scanned and included on your website.

CDs or inexpensive memory sticks will be suitable for examples of motion work, as will a link in an email to an online showreel loaded up to sites such as Vimeo or YouTube.

Accessibility/clarity

You may also consider short, well-placed captions in a physical folio. These will be important for commissioned pieces, and will differentiate them from mock-ups or speculative images.

There are many different types of folio available and you will find one that suits your financial means as well as the nature of your artwork. Be aware that many offices and design studios have limited space, so large folios could be impractical in these environments.

3 Alice Wellinger, *Irgendwo, irgendwann*, a children's book published by Verlag Bibliothek der Provinz, 2010. Alice took a rather unusual approach to her book projects.

I took a rather unusual approach: My books were individual projects – works without a contract. The text, pictures and layout were all mine. I sent the finished layout to publishers of children's books and that led to a long and frustrating odyssey. 'If at first you don't succeed, try and try again' – success came in the end as my books found a publisher and then they won some international awards as well.
Alice Wellinger

ORGANIZING
YOUR FOLIO
AND WEBSITE

AGENT
REPRESENTATION

VISUAL LITERACY

4

I try to give myself the kind of brief I like to receive when working commercially, which consists of guidelines to adhere to, but just enough freedom for me to develop creatively each time and perhaps push an idea to its furthest extent, with time permitting. Although, I really enjoy pursuing personal work as I feel this gives me the best chance to investigate new aesthetics that could later be incorporated into potential jobs. Each project will have its own guidelines in order for the finished image to achieve a visual target and to emulate a commercial job.
Stuart Whitton

4 Stuart Whitton, the title image of Stuart's solo exhibition, 'Origin'. It is important to strike a balance between personal and commercial projects.

Authorial attitude: personal work and potential commercial projects

Over the course of your career, personal work can sustain and feed into what you produce commercially, as well as keeping you fresh by continually expanding your skills base. Drawing and maintaining sketchbooks, as well as working on more substantial projects, allows you to explore evolving ideas and artwork with new subjects and approaches in contexts that your commercial practice doesn't always allow. Producing new samples to keep your folio up-to-date means that you have new promotion to send to clients and content to keep your blog current.

In some areas of illustration, taking an authorial approach is integral to practice. Typically, picture book illustrators and graphic novelists create dummy books often working with their own narrative, which they submit to publishers for consideration.

Greetings cards illustrators and character designers often work in a similar vein, creating sample designs suitable to be licensed into products which are then mass-produced or further developed and applied. Illustrators focusing on animation can send showreels to producers and animation studios. For authorial work, seek possible funding opportunities to finance projects.

As an illustrator operating in this way, your role is proactive – you are not selling your style to be applied to another commission but art directing yourself. This approach is often complementary to taking commissions. The slow burn of your own projects can bring balance to your practice, filling the gaps made by working to shorter commissions.

Although there is no guarantee that personal work will lead directly to paid commissions, the bonus of considering this work as a valid dimension of your practice can also provide a psychological lift and keep a momentum in your business during quieter periods.

We're always on the lookout for something eye-catching and original, but the story has to work in its own right. A beautifully produced dummy will capture our attention, but there's no point in creating something that looks stunning if the story isn't strong enough. I personally like miniature dummies – there's something very appealing about a mini book with lots of tiny details so that you discover more each time you look. But this wouldn't work for everything and really all (all!) we need to see is a strong idea and some great pictures – the rest can be developed with us.

We're sent hundreds of submissions, so it's worth putting in the extra effort to make sure your dummy stands out. Having said that, it certainly doesn't need to be final artwork, although it's good to see a sample of this. It's interesting, as well as useful, to get a glimpse into the illustrator's creative process, to see a combination of rough sketches, black and white line and finished colour. Editors are used to seeing the different stages of development and it can be off-putting to receive something with 'final' stamped across it, as it suggests the illustrator isn't interested in feedback and suggestions. As well as looking for talented writers and illustrators, we're looking for people we'll enjoy working with, and who will enjoy working with us – it's very much a collaborative process.

If you're sending a dummy, we only need a short, simple covering letter – there's no need to give a detailed description when we can see the book for ourselves!
Hannah Featherstone,
David Fickling Books

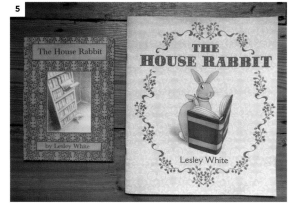

5 Lesley White, dummy books for *The House Rabbit*, published by Fickling Books.

ORGANIZING
YOUR FOLIO
AND WEBSITE

AGENT
REPRESENTATION

VISUAL LITERACY

6 Mario Minichiello, 'Irish Bar, Sydney', personal drawing. Self-initiated work such as this can help illustrators to develop their own processes and style.

Developing personal work also helps you to break out of a creative rut, change direction or try out new ideas. I have found that the best means to develop these personal moments of experimentation, authorship and of testing your authorial voice is in the sketchbook. This is a private space where you can remake experiences (remediation) into visual constructions that can be communicated to others and you can refine your visual vocabulary. This system of remediation is inherent in drawing but it has to be practised, just as a dancer, or boxer has to practise their key attributes, so do you. This helps to distinguish what we do as illustrators from the work of others who provide the world with images, such as photographers or painters.

Professor Mario Minichiello
The University of Newcastle, Australia

Commercial outlets

Increasingly, commissioned illustrators are optimizing and creating new potential commercial outlets for personally generated, authorial work. Many websites now include online shops, and websites such as *Etsy*, *notonthehighstreet.com* and *Society6* are legitimate commercial avenues. Typical outlets include:

- Products where imagery has been applied decoratively as surface pattern – this could include wallpapers, ceramics, skins for tablets and phones, bags and wall stickers.

- Limited edition prints.

- Pieces of original artwork.

- Toys.

- Limited edition publications; zines, comics and books.

- Stationery items; greetings cards, calendars and gift wrap.

- Textiles; fabrics and T-shirts.

- Apps and screen savers.

The production of some of these will require financial outlay, so market research and costings should be undertaken before investment of time or money is made. Distribution costs should be factored in, whether this would entail post and packaging or time and expenses incurred through approaching retail outlets directly.

7

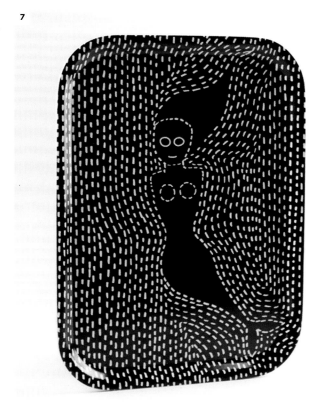

7 Tyra van Zweigbergk, tray design.

8

8 Zara Wood aka Woody, T-shirt design for Topshop.

ORGANIZING
YOUR FOLIO
AND WEBSITE

AGENT
REPRESENTATION

VISUAL LITERACY

9

9 Tad Carpenter, an illustration and art print for National Bike month.

AGENT REPRESENTATION

Developing platforms through which your work will be seen and ensuring that they evolve and are relevant commercially should be ongoing. For some artists, agent representation or business partnerships perform a valuable service, but it is important to be aware of the pros and cons of operating in this way.

If your work is marketable and you are beginning to gain regular commissions, you may consider seeking agent representation so that you can focus predominantly on the creative dimension of your business. Although the nature and size of illustration agencies differs, there is a generic service offered and they operate along similar lines.

Generally, an agency comprises a specialist team dedicated to the promotion of the artists they represent, increasingly within an international market. They act as the conduit between you as an artist and your clients: taking the brief, negotiating licences, fees and organizing payments. In exchange they take a commission, approximately 30% of the fees that they earn for you. Each commission through the agency should have a written brief with delivery dates for visuals and final artwork, plus any special considerations.

You retain your copyright as an artist, although your agent may be entitled to a percentage of your ongoing royalties from certain types of commissions. The agency/artist relationship is a mutual one; both sides are working together for the benefit of each other, and it is an equal partnership.

Larger agencies have specialist staff who focus on particular areas of the field, such as motion, children's publishing and concept art. There are specialist agencies that focus entirely on promoting illustrators working in these areas as well as literary agents who represent only picture book illustrators and author/illustrators.

It's a good entry point, but what really sells me on an artist is seeing someone who is incredibly prolific. They create because they have to, and have a variety of different avenues that they express themselves. Whether it is through design, photography, self-initiated projects, community involvement, etc. – anything that results in some consistent body of visual content and really provides a good understanding of who they are as a person and how they experience the creative process. On the flip side, there are definitely many things that favour a more restrained approach. There are so many occasions where an art director will pick one artist over another because they have an existing piece of work that more closely fits the exact nature of the brief. To that end, we prefer artists with a deeper well to draw from as it just makes our job easier and increases their chances of securing the job.
Jeremy Wortsman, The Jacky Winter Group, Australia

10 Marcela Restrepo, 'Notebook – Love', an illustration for the 2011 Sydney Festival identity. Marcela is represented by The Jacky Winter Group.

10

Agent pros

A good agent has up-to-date industry knowledge, extensive databases and established relationships with high-profile clients. They know where to pitch your work and should have more opportunities and invitations to show your folio than you as an individual would.

They have extensive marketing knowledge, established mechanisms for promotion, such as websites, visibility at trade fairs and presence in source books, and seek wide exposure for those they represent. They have extensive experience of contracts and copyright matters and skill in negotiating higher fees.

An agent will recognize the commercial potential in your artwork and work with you to develop, optimize and direct your portfolio accordingly.

11 Natsko Seki, poster for Yebisu Garden Place, Tokyo. Natsko has been represented by a number of agencies.

I have been represented by agents Taiko & Associates, Tokyo, and AgencyRush, UK. Working with agencies is good, especially when the clients are too big to deal with by myself. It means I avoid having to face potential problems such as copyright, and also negotiating fees.
Natsko Seki

Agent cons

Being represented does not guarantee commissions – if you hand over all responsibility for marketing your work to an agent, your promotion could lose its momentum and your own database and client contacts may become dated. Being recognized within an agency for a specific type of work can result in you being put forward repeatedly for similar types of commission. Over time this could restrict your practice.

Having an agent means that both illustrators and clients miss out on the personal interaction that can result from the briefing process. Some briefs can evolve and expand because of the professional rapport and dynamic that occurs when an illustrator works closely with a commissioning client. Also, if you are part of a stable of artists, you may not all have the agency's full attention.

I do not work with an agent, although I think they can be useful for different markets, such as book publishing and foreign markets. I work for many visible publications and have been fortunate to consistently have work in various annuals and shows.
Ellen Weinstein

12 Ellen Weinstein, 'The Unbelievers', an illustration for *The New York Times* style section. Ellen is not represented by an agent.

Agency terms

All business relationships benefit from clarity in what is expected from each participant in the relationship. So, in the same way that illustrators want to have a clear understanding of how a commission will operate with a client, they should also know what they expect from an agent, and what the agency expects from them.

An artist may be represented by an agency and additionally retain their own separate clients, but increasingly agencies ask that if signed to the agency the artist will exclusively accept commissions through them and refer any approaches on to the agent to handle. This exclusivity is usually within the agent's country. You need to be happy with such an arrangement – if not, discuss it with them. Some agencies are active abroad so you would have to establish whether you could be represented by different agents in other territories. If an agreement is signed then both sides need to be clear that they must abide by it.

Promotion, as for individuals, is an essential part of an agency's strategy, and there will be a timetable for promotion throughout the year. This may take the form of mail-outs, inclusion in the agency's publications and source books, the agency's site and portfolio websites, e-newsletters and special promotions. The cost for materials, printing, postage and web fees is usually divided between the agency and those it represents. How much this will cost the artist as a percentage of the overall costs, and how payment will be met, should be specified in the agency's agreement. You will need to know if you will be asked for money upfront or whether sums due can be deducted from future commission fees.

Not all agency relationships continue to blossom over time – work may dry up for various reasons, the artist may want to take a new direction that the agent does not support, or the relationship may deteriorate. For this reason, there should always be a termination clause in the agreement which details how this separation of business proceeds. For example, can you approach clients that were introduced to you by the agency as soon as you have left?

Each commission we produce adds knowledge and experience into our bank, and whenever we handle a commission, we are able to refer back on that rich source of information. Where a successful artist may only have a few dozen jobs to draw from, we are coming from a background of thousands. The good ones and the bad ones. We're like navigators in that we know all the different places jobs come from and which ways they can go. It's like a weird and wonderful road trip.
Jeremy Wortsman – director, The Jacky Winter Group, Australia

Agent/illustrator relationship

Although you don't need to be best friends with your agent, it is important that you have a positive rapport with them. You should be confident that they understand your artwork and working process, what areas of the industry you are comfortable working in, and what ambitions you have for the future in terms of expanding your client base or the direction of your artwork. They should be supportive of their artists, acting as a buffer between artist and client if required, should a commission not go smoothly.

Communication is important. Keep in touch with the agency, ensuring that they are kept up-to-date with any new work and personal projects. Regular contact by email, phone or a meet-up, even if it is just to say hello, keeps you in mind. Take the initiative; constantly review how things are working, and if you'd like to work for specific brands, or broaden your scope, then let it be known.

Many areas in the illustration industry, such as advertising, move rapidly and it can be important to respond promptly to requests from your agent. Opportunities can be lost if the agent is unable to provide a swift solution to a client's wishes.

Transparency in dealings is important; agents should ensure that their artists receive paperwork relating to each commission, covering items such as the fee achieved, the rights licensed to the client, the date invoiced, the delivery dates for visuals and final artwork, as well as any special considerations. Artists should also expect regular statements throughout the year from the agency on money due, paid and owing (for promotion).

New business models

Other options exist that can suit creative individuals, such as partnerships and collectives. Groups of creatives can offer many of the benefits of an agent, drawing on pooled knowledge of pricing commissions, dealing with contracts, acting as general advisors and offering companionship and encouragement. The different skill sets of members can be utilized for the benefit of all involved, and members can share contacts and divide costs of promotion. Skills can be matched up for the benefit of clients, allowing the group to offer more than the individuals can on his or her own. These set-ups also encourage collaborations between artists, especially if they are occupying a shared space, with familiarity offering an ease of communication. Group exhibitions by a collective can take advantage of numbers by exhibiting in larger spaces than an individual could afford, enhancing the overall impact.

New business models continue to develop with a growing number of illustrators working with a non-creative partner, which allows them to concentrate on the creation of artwork and participation in exhibitions whilst the partner organizes the business side. As with collectives, this is also a solution to the isolation that artists can sometimes experience when working on their own.

13

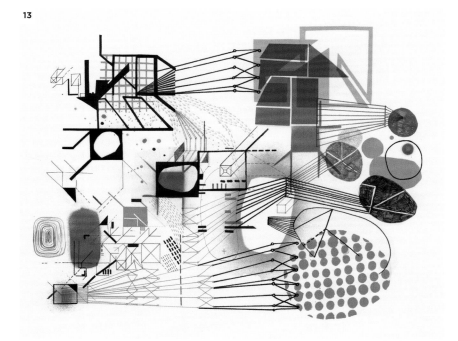

13 James Gulliver Hancock, semi-abstract illustrations for *Always Building*, a philosophical book by Herman Miller. James is represented by The Jacky Winter Group.

AN ILLUSTRATOR WITH AGENT REPRESENTATION: ULLA PUGGAARD

Ulla Puggaard is represented by several agents in different territories – Kate Larkworthy in the USA, CIA (Central Illustration Agency) in the UK and Europe, and Tomorrow Management in her native Denmark – and while it is not uncommon for artists to have representation in different countries, Ulla's agency connections have developed gradually through her career. She was already with Kate Larkworthy before signing with CIA, and wanted to maintain Kate's close connections in the USA – rather than have CIA take over that territory.

An artist with a strong graphic background, Ulla also works as a designer and her clear, bold style is commissioned across the advertising, publishing and editorial fields. She maintains a good relationship with her agents: 'I'm always able to call them, have discussions around work, where to push for new things, or what to select to show. I use my agents as much as I can.' She believes there should be a certain chemistry between artist and agent: 'My agents understand how my work is created, and how to get the best work conditions for me.' Not all illustrators will suit being represented, and she says that artists need to feel that they are valued.

The relationship with clients is vital to Ulla, and although not all agencies will operate this way, she asks that once the general brief, fees, timescale and rights have been negotiated by her agent she is put directly in touch with the client: 'I enjoy getting to know art directors. That's a good thing, as there's no interference in the actual creative process. So unless something is going wrong, and the agent needs to step in, you just get on with it.' With a busy work schedule, Ulla acknowledges that having someone to deal with the non-artistic practical side of a commission is very useful. Time can be spent on the artwork and the agent can work on areas such as negotiating a better fee if more time is taken to complete the job than originally anticipated.

As an illustrator, she feels supported by the agencies – for them the artist is the main priority. They want it to work for both sides, and will not try to push an inappropriate job on her. On the other hand, if they don't consider the job to be worthy they will still present her with the option of choosing to take it on. She values CIA's attitude to promotion: 'They try to find the most efficient way to do it, so it doesn't cost us too much to be part of it', and also appreciates that areas of promotion that she lacks the time to embrace, such as social media, can be covered by those with the relevant expertise within the agency.

Development for an artist is important, and agencies will remind their illustrators that it is time to update their portfolio, 'but,' Ulla stresses, 'it's up to the individual to keep that appetite, and keep doing new work.' She has found that the agency will be honest about whether a new approach is going to be commercially viable in their view.

Ulla makes the most of being represented, but believes: 'You can't rely on the agent to sort everything out for you anyway, so I've always chosen to take an active approach.'

1

The Pen That Never Forgets

Could a pen that records sound while you write be the key to taking good notes?

By Clive Thompson

LETTERING BY ULLA PUGGAARD

The Pen
That Never
Forgets

Could a pen
that records sound
while you write
be the key to taking
good notes?

2

3

1 'The Pen That Never Forgets', a typographic illustration for *The New York Times*.
2 Ulla's page on her agent's (Central Illustration Agency) website.
3 Promotional items from CIA. Some of Ulla's work is included here: *Licence to Inspire*, published by Pirum Press, 'Alternative Games' 2012 calendar, 'Keyhole' and 'No Sin' prints. All of these are also sold through CIA's online shop.

AN ILLUSTRATOR WITHOUT AGENT REPRESENTATION: TAD CARPENTER

Working without agent representation does not stop Tad Carpenter from working successfully for a diverse and constant stream of clients across many applications of illustration. His witty images and characters have been commissioned for a myriad of international clients, such as Macy's, Atlantic Records, MTV, Hallmark Cards, and Kidrobot and he has had children's books published as author/illustrator: 'Despite the extra amount of work, I like being able to represent myself. At times it might be easier to have someone else do it but I like that when a client calls they are talking directly to me.'

Versatility is important. The illustration skills manifest through this work are complemented by his confidence as a designer and some of his success can be attributed to the ability to handle a job in its entirety from conception through to artwork: 'In our current design you are a visual communicator as opposed to just an illustrator or graphic designer. So many of us are wearing multiple hats. The diversification of the work motivates me.'

Tad's independent approach undoubtedly relies upon his strength as an entrepreneur who seeks new challenges and puts in long hours to achieve them. In addition to attracting an array of clients, he is excited by licensing his own products. He reflects on his direction of Vahalla Studios, which specializes in silk-screen goods, creating limited edition illustration products and artefacts such as gig posters and invites, sometimes to be sold through his shop or for galleries and events: 'The work not necessarily for a client allows me to explore and play. It is always important to remember what we do is something that we love. We must remember to play, experiment. When we make for no reason other than to make, we can find all sorts of unexpected gains.'

The work generated in this more authorial capacity complements commercial assignments and can stimulate further print-based commissions, such as the associated assignments he has achieved for clients including MySpace, Rayban and Polo.

Although no longer touting for work he is anything but complacent: 'I have been lucky that of late I have been approached about potential and future projects. I am starting to write and illustrate children's books more and more and I do approach publishers on book concepts.' Juggling commissions is complemented by managing all aspects of running this multifaceted business, including promotion. Tad relies mostly on generic illustration platforms as well as managing his own custom-built site, reflecting, 'It is being part designer and part salesman.'

He clearly recognizes the investment gained from building and sustaining the personal relationship with clients that can't be so easily achieved through agent representation: 'On occasion I send silk-screen prints to clients as thank yous: at the end of the year I send out silk-screen holiday goodies such as cards and prints, and a custom-made board game and pieces.'

Dealing with the business aspects of his practice is something Tad describes as, 'always a work in progress.' Operating without an agent to do the negotiating of terms over such a range of briefs presents obvious challenges: 'Still, after several years, I feel I am just starting to get my feet under me when it comes to the business end of art direction, design and illustration. Understanding your rights as an artist is one of the most important things we can all do.' He proves the importance for independent artists to recognize a network of reliable support: 'I continually lean on the *Graphic Artist's Guild Handbook: Pricing and Ethical Guidelines,* which gives us all a good place to start when it comes to pricing and ownership of your work.'

Tad shows that ultimately, working without an agent requires a package of skills that includes confidence: 'The main advice I have is trust yourself. If you have a vision, if you have a look, follow it. Make what you want to make and get it out there. People will see it and start to hire you to do what you do.'

1, 2 Branding and promotional badges for Yeah! Burger, a new restaurant concept. Illustrations were created for 2D and 3D application.
3 Snowboard design for Zion's Woah! Man 2012 series.

NEW BUSINESS MODELS:
HARTWIG BRAUN AND ISAAC LILOS

Hartwig Braun and Isaac Lilos's successful business partnership evolved from a personal relationship in 2005. Before Isaac's intervention, Hartwig was an architect who considered his drawing activities to be, 'merely a hobby.' Isaac's encouragement and 'pestering' was instrumental in his partner's creative development, helping him to realize his fuller potential as a successful illustrator.

Their collaborative partnership is a synthesis of Hartwig's now mature, confident and award-winning approach to image-making and Isaac's commercial acumen. This accrued not from managing other artists but from his being an entrepreneur, 'from being involved in various family businesses and having my own ventures along the way, which gave me a wealth of knowledge, experience and skills about how to start, grow and manage a business effectively.'

The business flourishes as a result of their focus on shared long-term objectives that optimize their complementary, individual abilities. Isaac clarifies: 'Hartwig and I balance each other in a good way', he adds, 'Agents might sometimes be tempted to pursue opportunities just because of their financial or commercial gains. For us as a partnership it is much more important to develop Hartwig's profile as an artist and our Arty Globe brand in the right way – even if it means sometimes saying no to very lucrative opportunities, which do not fit in with our long-term goal and vision.'

Those aspects of the illustration business that can seem daunting to an individual practitioner are skillfully negotiated by Isaac: 'Through my experiences I have learnt how important it is to be assertive and persistent. I discovered my natural networking skills and my tenacious nature to persist despite getting an initial "no" as an answer or be faced with big problems and challenges.'

Ensuring that Hartwig is effectively promoted is a priority: their aim is to reach the right people at the appropriate time: 'Metaphorically you can say that I have a natural talent for spotting the right doors to knock on and the cheek and assertiveness to knock on them to get them opened. Hartwig's work is unique enough to attract attention and keep the doors open.'

Although the success of the business is important for each of them, Isaac is able to bring a more detached and often pragmatic perspective to the commercial aspects of a commission or project: 'I can talk about Hartwig's work in ways that he may not.' Being in this more objective position has ramifications when negotiating fees: 'I know this is normally the case with agents as well, but I think that in a partnership this becomes even more important where both people have vested interest in getting the best possible deal.' Hartwig is able to focus on the creative process which is the heart of the business, liaising with the clients when necessary and producing the artwork which is pivotal to each partner's success.

Unlike agency representation, Hartwig enjoys being the sole artist in Isaac's business focus: 'A partnership like ours is a lot more involved than just a formal agency relationship. As full-time professional (and personal) partners, we can work a lot closer to achieve much more together.'

1 'London in Tea', an example of Hartwig's popular urban drawings. This image has subsequently been used on a number of products such as tableware and clothing.

CHAPTER FIVE
SECURING WORK

In the early stages of your career, being approached by a client offering you a commission can be an exciting but also daunting experience. Whether you are contacted by email, via telephone or briefed during a folio showing, whatever the content or nature of the brief, whatever the scale of the job, it pays to remember that this is a business transaction. Talking business is a two-way process of interaction between you and the client; you are not a passive party.

There are practical steps to take that will ensure that the communication in the briefing situation is appropriate and that the process goes smoothly. Irrespective of your personality, how shy or confident you are when interacting with other people, you can learn to be efficient in dealing with clients.

Rob Hodgson

THE STAGES OF FORMING A CONTRACT

The offer

The first stage of forming a contract occurs when the illustrator is approached by the client. Once this offer has been made, it is then considered and/or negotiated and then accepted or declined.

Increasingly, you will be briefed via telephone and email. Although the process may seem informal, it is important to acknowledge that being approached with a commission is the first step in a legal process. Some clients will be very experienced and thorough in clearly outlining what is required, others will be less rigorous. For this reason you need to be aware of, and responsible for, finding out firstly what is required of you and secondly under what terms you will be expected to operate. Although there are areas of common practice across the profession, it is not safe to presume that there are standard principles that will be automatically implemented.

Recognizing what information you require, establishing a checklist if necessary and being diligent with recording what has been negotiated will guarantee that you handle the process effectively.

Don't be afraid to ask if you need something specific, be it information, clarity on the brief or a bigger fee. The onus is upon you to be sufficiently informed to undertake the commission and meet the client's requirements.
Zachariah OHora

1 Zachariah OHora, illustration for the picture book *The Pet Project*, by Lisa Wheeler, published by Simon & Schuster.

The following list of questions will help you during this process:

What are you being asked to do?

Who is the overall client? (If your commissioner is a design or advertising agency, it is likely they will have a client commissioning them.)

Where will the image be used?

Who is the intended audience?

What will the function of the image be?

What are the qualities the client is looking for – is there a particular piece of your artwork that they are referring to?

What is the visual approach that is required?

What technical considerations are there?

What is the number of images?

What size will they be reproduced at, and what scale should your artwork be created to?

Are they full colour or black and white?

Are there media considerations (such as identifying where processes or cut-outs could be used in greetings cards)?

Do you provide the photograph if your work is 3D?

In what format will they require final artwork and at what resolution?

What is the process?

Do they want to approve a visual before artwork stage?

Do they want you to speak to their client for direct briefing?

What are the deadlines for each aspect of the process?

Are there other illustrators pitching for the same job?

What are the terms under which you are producing the work?

How much will you get paid?

What form will this fee take – a one-off fee or royalties?

How long will your licence for the use of the artwork be for?

Where will the work be published?

Consideration/negotiation

Negotiation is the aspect of the briefing process that illustrators can find most difficult.

There can be awkwardness around negotiating fees, ignorance about rights and copyright in the artwork and a general fear of jeopardizing future commissions by being anything other than compliant with all that is proposed.

Before accepting any commission, establish that all the information that you need to proceed has been provided and ensure that you are satisfied with what is offered. You may need to negotiate a bigger fee, more time or clarify some aspect of what has been offered, and there may be a series of new offers made by the client as a result of this negotiation. You may require time to consider what has been offered before you commit to the commission.

If there are aspects you want to change, it is important to make the client aware of them before you accept and before you start work on the commission. At this stage you need to be thorough and clear, giving your client time to consider whatever you propose. Being assertive about your requirements may be necessary and there are strategies you can adopt to tactically renegotiate.

Ask for time to consider what has been offered and let the client know when you will contact them with a response. Consulting with more experienced peers, your subject's trade association or thinking through what you have been offered may provide you with a clearer view of how to proceed. This shouldn't jeopardize the commission. Adopting a professional manner and being prompt in your subsequent reply, clearly outlining any areas for negotiation, is standard practice.

The more informed you are about the profession, the more likely you will be able to gauge whether what you are being offered is a good deal, and if not, how to proceed.

If you know your rights, you will be more confident about bargaining around them when necessary. This means having a clear understanding of what it means to own the copyright in your work.

Be honest about your personal position. If you are busy and a commission doesn't fit immediately within your work schedule, see if an alternative deadline can be negotiated. If you think the fees or proposed usage of the artwork being offered is unreasonable, state your alternative or preferred terms in a direct and professional manner. You must be prepared to ultimately make a decision whether to proceed based on the client's response to your requests. Sometimes illustrators have to decline commissions and clients are prepared for this.

2

It is very important to find out as much information from the client before you start drawing, i.e. which examples of your work they like, any specific elements that must be featured in the illustration and schedule for delivery of the work.
Harriet Taylor Seed

2 Harriet Taylor Seed, downloadable wallpaper for Folk Wallpaper The Fox is Black, an art and design blog: www.thefoxisblack.com.

Acceptance

When you have agreed to undertake the commission, both parties are bound by the terms of acceptance. Subsequently, neither you nor your client is legally entitled to alter any of the conditions. Some clients have formal agreements that will be provided automatically at the outset in the form of a contract or purchase order. If you work in publishing, there are agreement models that contain standard clauses that are adapted to suit each commission.

You may not be automatically offered a written brief prior to commencing the commission, and if this is the case you must ensure that some form of written agreement is sent to the client. This can be your own 'acceptance of commission' form detailing all aspects of the job (see page 181 for a same form).

Alternatively, a summary of the points raised during the briefing session and the fees agreed should be emailed to the client once the job is accepted in order to to avoid any subsequent misinterpretation from either party. This can take the form of an email covering all the necessary points, but a formal attached document is more professional, and a more efficient form of business record.

Every contract should have details of the usage, duration and territory along with a description of the work you have been asked to produce.

Budgets and deadlines are often negotiable (within reason) so being armed with the knowledge of what a half page/full page/cover image or even billboard should be worth will allow you to approach the negotiation in a confident and objective manner. This is a day-to-day part of being an illustrator and being clear and politely concise about your requirements will be respected and ensure you get the full value from your work.
Mark Smith

3 Mark Smith, 'Where Are All of the Gay Athletes?', illustration for *ESPN* magazine.

THE TERMS OF AN AGREEMENT

You might assume that each agreement you are given is for that commission only, but some will contain wording that defines a contract as covering the current and all future commissions for that commissioning organization.

All rights

If 'all rights' appears in an agreement from a commissioner, it is important that this is defined between you and your client. They may interpret the phrase to imply an assignment of copyright – but an 'all rights' licence should be defined as meaning that the client is requesting to be able to use the artwork in all media.

Cancellation fees

These should be paid when the job is cancelled by the client with no fault attached to the illustrator. A good guide is 25% of the agreed fee before visuals stage; 33% on delivery of visuals; 100% on delivery of final artwork stage.

4 Anna Steinberg, 'Business Survival Boat', an illustration for Creative Choices website, helping creatives to develop their careers: www.creative-choices.co.uk.

THE STAGES
OF FORMING A
CONTRACT

**THE TERMS OF
AN AGREEMENT**

WHO OWNS
THE RIGHTS?

Rejection fees

These are paid when the client decides the artwork does not come up to the standard expected of the illustrator. The standard payments are 25% of the agreed fee at rough stage, and 50% at finished artwork stage.

Always read contracts... but also, be informed about what the small print means, because that's a part of your job. And if it's appalling nonsense, challenge it. (As opposed to reading it, not agreeing and signing it anyway.)
Anna Steinberg

Licences

A licence is an agreement between you and your client, which allows them to reproduce your images. It defines what the client can do with the images, for how long, and in which territories.

The elements that make up a licence are the rights you are giving the client in your artwork, and are defined as:

Usage – how the image is to be used by the client (this can be multiple uses).

Duration – the length of time the client wants to use the image for.

Territory – where the product will be used/sold.

Your artwork is being commissioned for certain usages (for example, to be applied as character design for an app, drinks packaging or wrapping paper); for use for a certain length of time (for example, six months, five years or for the period of copyright); and in a defined territory (for example, USA only, UK only, all European countries or worldwide).

To work out what fee you should charge your client, you will need this information from them.

If the client is unsure how long they wish to license your work for, a long licence with an appropriate fee should be negotiated. If they have not defined what usages they need or what territory they want to cover, then they should request a licence that covers all possible eventualities. In this instance, an 'all media licence, worldwide' will cover this, although it should come with a substantial fee.

Most clients will want the work you do for them to be exclusive to their company. This means that the images you create for them are for their use only, and you will not be able to licence those images to anyone else until the license you have granted to them has expired. However, exclusivity can be requested for just a certain area, so you could license an image to your client for use exclusively only within the giftware industry, but still be able to license it outside that area, in publishing or editorially, for example.

Below are some examples of how licences influence the fee:

- A licence to use an illustration on 1,000 T-shirts for a small one-off festival will be less than a design used for T-shirts for a global fashion store with a run of 10,000 garments.

- An image for two months, use on a local hairdresser's promotional flyer will attract a smaller fee than a licence for use on a national bank's in-store leaflet for the duration of a one-year licence period.

- An illustration to feature on a nationwide billboard advertising campaign will command a higher fee than one for a smaller territory, such as a single city.

Licensing, additional licences and re-licences

A licence can include multiple uses for an image. A licence for a character design may include its use over a range of products, applications and even platforms. Once a licence has expired, you are free to sell the image to anyone else or use it within your own products. This is called re-licensing. You can benefit from re-licensing in particular if your work is suitable to be used for alternative uses than the original or within other territories. If you license yourself through your agent's or your own website, you can continue to assert some control over its use and set or influence the fee.

Stock libraries

Your back catalogue has an inherent resale value and some artists choose to sell their rights, for variable rates of pay, through stock libraries. There are varying models but the general principle is to make existing imagery available for reuse for a set fee.

Stock companies have been criticized for undermining the profession, both in terms of how illustration is used and in eroding the fee structure by supplying the market with cheap, generic imagery. Stock sold for minimal prices across all areas of the profession has an impact on the amount of bespoke illustration commissioned, so ultimately could be counterproductive for illustrators.

As an illustrator, if you hand over your work to a stock agency, you relinquish control of who your images are sold to and in what context they are used.

How will I quote and negotiate fees and prices?

You have been asked by a client to create artwork for their use, and you are entitled to a fee in exchange for the right to reproduce your images. The fees for different commissions will vary, and are based on usage, duration and territory. Generally speaking, the larger the use, the longer the time it is to be used and the greater the size of the territory, the higher the fee.

Clients will have a financial budget for their required illustration – what they are ultimately prepared to pay for artwork. You are rarely offered this information, and so the sum you quote for a job will always be compared to this budget. If your quote comes in higher than the budget, a negotiating situation will arise where the client will try to reduce your proposed fee.

5

5 Beth Pountney, 'Shiver Me Timbers', an illustration now used in art prints.

I license my designs with a variety of usage, such as ceramics, cards, giftware, packaging and children's merchandise and also work with publishers illustrating children's board books. As well as working with larger companies, I sell work directly to the public through my website, other consumer gift sites and giftware fairs. I find that by selling directly to the public, I am able to keep up to date with what people want.
Beth Pountney

I learned about licences, copyright and fees with on-the-job training. I have colleagues I can discuss these matters with and I am also active within the illustration community, I am on the boards of ICON7: The Illustration Conference, and the Society of Illustrators. These topics are constantly evolving with the introduction of new media and usage. It is important to be informed and work to maintain fees or else everyone's ability to earn a living through our work is eroded.
Ellen Weinstein

THE STAGES
OF FORMING A
CONTRACT

**THE TERMS OF
AN AGREEMENT**

WHO OWNS
THE RIGHTS??

6 Ellen Weinstein,
'The Power of Communities',
an editorial illustration
published in *Harvard Law
Review*.

6

Payment

Income from artwork fees can be supplied in several ways:

A flat fee. This is a one-off payment applied to most commissions.

A royalty. This is based on a percentage of sales of an item, for example an app, book, toy or card. A royalty is based on future sales, so it is desirable to receive an upfront payment for the creation of your artwork in the form of an advance on royalties. As sales, and therefore royalty payments, cannot be guaranteed, it is important that the sum of the advance is sufficient to cover your time and expenses.

Royalty agreements can contain a substantial number of clauses, especially for books, and will cover digital rights, sub-licensing rights to other publishers, translation and foreign rights, merchandising rights and termination of contract.

An hourly rate. You may be asked by a potential client what your 'day rate' is. But note that usage for an illustration should never be based on how long it has taken for you to create the artwork. A rate based on time can be applied to situations where you may be required to do additional work on a project that was not anticipated during quotation of the original fee. For more details on rates see Chapter 6.

Royalty payments

Royalty payments from licensing agreements or book sales will continue until the agreement expires. If this is a long time period, such as with many book deals, be aware that if you have an agent your agreement with them may state that even if either party terminates the agency contract, they continue to receive a percentage of those royalty payments on ongoing arrangements made through the agency. You may wish to negotiate a time period at which this agreement expires, should you leave an agency.

I sell a few reproductions and originals myself on Etsy but otherwise I'm not responsible for anything to do with the sales and distribution of commissioned work, that is the work of my clients. I have learned about fees over time... and from talking to my fellow artists. Not accepting royalties below 6% is the most important rule!
Adolie Day

7 Adolie Day, cut-out character. An example of a piece Adolie produced for a fixed fee rather than royalties.

THE STAGES
OF FORMING A
CONTRACT

THE TERMS OF
AN AGREEMENT

WHO OWNS
THE RIGHTS?

8

I distinguish between three types of customer: Firstly, the 'freebie': family and friends expect you to work for free and I'm (mostly) happy to do this. Then there are the 'Thanks, but no thanks' customers. The ones who contact you and say, 'We can't pay you much for this job because we have a really limited budget but there are more jobs in the pipeline…' Forget it! You'll never hear from this type of customer again after you complete the job. Be wary of 'friends of friends', too! They might praise your work to high heaven, but that doesn't mean you'll be rewarded with more than a box of chocolates in the end.

Thirdly, we have the 'perfect clients'. Really good clients know how valuable the work of a good illustrator is. They offer a decent fee right from the start, so no awkward price negotiations are necessary. If you can, work only with professionals – it will save you a lot of trouble. In general I set my fees based on what I hear about my colleagues' pricing and the calculations guidelines issued by my local subject association.
Alice Wellinger

8 Alice Wellinger, 'Blossfeldt's Dog', personal work. This image was selected to appear in the Society of Illustrators Annual.

WHO OWNS THE RIGHTS?

Understanding any agreements supplied by your client is important. They can be in unfamiliar language and some, such as royalty contracts, could be very long. It may be tempting to scan what appears to be impenetrable legal jargon and conclude that as you will never understand it, you might as well sign it regardless. This puts you at a disadvantage, and may mean you are giving the client rights you did not intend to hand over. Make the effort to comprehend the details, and if you still cannot follow them satisfactorily, ask your client to explain what is included in the agreement. If your art director is unable to clarify the terms, they should be able to put you on to someone in the organization who can.

It can be easy for both you and your client to assume that what you or they want from this agreement has been agreed if it is not put in writing, when in fact it is not necessarily clear to both parties. Assumptions can be made, and misunderstandings may then arise.

You own all the rights in your work until you license them to a client, and controlling your rights is the way you generate income as a freelancing artist. Some clients may not have a thorough comprehension of your rights. They may mistakenly assume that as they have paid you to make some artwork that they own the physical work (if it exists) and the right to use it however they please.

If you supply work physically rather than digitally, remember that ownership of artwork is separate from the right to reproduce it. You can still own the original artwork and assign rights in the image to another person; or sell the artwork but retain the right to reproduce it. You may find yourself in the position of having to explain licensing and ownership of original artwork to them.

The wording of a supplied contract may not exactly follow that of your brief – clients may attempt to get more rights in your work than they have originally asked for, so check that you agree everything before signing. USA contracts containing the phrase 'work for hire' means that the copyright in the work you create will be owned by the client.

Negotiating fees for artwork can be hard, especially as different usage, size of artwork and the amount of work required to produce the final image (which varies depending on how much information needs to go in the final image) all affect the pricing. I've found having an agent particularly helpful in pricing more complicated briefs; however, if you're working on your own, getting as much information as possible from the client is essential.
Kate Evans

I was so excited about getting my first picture book in the early 1990s that I didn't ensure that all the percentages in the contract were favourable to me. Twenty years later, it's still in print, but the income I receive from royalties is less than it would be if the contract had been negotiated to include a higher percentage. I'm reminded about this twice a year when my royalty statements arrive.
Derek Brazell

THE STAGES
OF FORMING A
CONTRACT

THE TERMS OF
AN AGREEMENT

**WHO OWNS
THE RIGHTS?**

9

9 Kate Evans, 'Budapest', book jacket for *Blue River, Black Sea* by Andrew Eames, published by Transworld Publishers.

10 Derek Brazell, *Cleversticks*, illustrated children's book published by HarperCollins.

10

Copyright and illustrators' ethics

Copyright is the right to copy. It comes into existence as soon as you create an artwork, draw a doodle, take a photograph or write some text, and it means that you are able to control how your work is reproduced (copied) and who can reproduce it. Copyright applies to both published and unpublished work, and lasts for the lifetime of the creator plus 70 years following his or her death. Copyright does not apply to ideas or styles.

Reproduction of your artwork is the means by which you generate income, and it is therefore a crucial right to control. As the copyright owner in your work, you are offering your client the right to reproduce the image they have commissioned in return for a fee. If, instead of giving a specific licence, copyright is assigned to a client, you lose control of that work and can no longer generate income from it through further licensing. This may be acceptable if the client proposes a sufficiently large fee for ownership of the copyright, but generally they do not. A licence is nearly always adequate for their requirements.

Copyright applies to all visual artists' work, so do not assume that you can take a photograph or artwork from any source, be it from an obscure book or an Internet site, and either incorporate the whole image, or a substantial part of it, in your artwork. Doing a drawing of a photograph, flipping an image, or using a significant part of it, is still an infringement of the creator's copyright. Artists and their commissioners increasingly showcase their new projects to the world via the Internet so it is unsafe to presume an infringement will go unseen. Considered use of work for reference, rather than direct copying, is permissible.

You may find yourself in the position where a client has given you some reference material or shown you another artist's work and asked you to create something 'just like this'. In both these situations you may be infringing the copyright of the creator of those images, and you, along with the client, would be liable for prosecution for infringement if discovered. Everyone who participates in an infringement is legally liable. Should you be asked to copy something and you are concerned, ask the client to indemnify you against any claims arising from your use of material supplied by the client.

Any work created under regular employment is considered the copyright of the employer, not the employee. The copyright for artwork created under a USA work-for-hire agreement is owned by the commissioner.

If you become aware that another party has used your artwork without your agreement or payment of a fee, this is infringement of your copyright and you can pursue for compensatory payment.

THE STAGES
OF FORMING A
CONTRACT

THE TERMS OF
AN AGREEMENT

WHO OWNS
THE RIGHTS?

133

When I need reference I'll work with either my own photographs or use several sources to ensure I'm making something unique to me.
Rebecca Abell

11, 12 Rebecca Abell, window display on boards and glass, Browns store, London.

Moral rights

Moral rights are separate from copyright, and are concerned with protection of your reputation as a creator and are applied differently in different countries. Moral rights protect your artwork from unapproved, unsuitable changes, therefore safeguarding your reputation, your right to be credited and the right not to have your name put to another's image.

Depending on which country you live in, there may be some variation in your rights. European moral rights are generally stronger than those in the UK. National government websites generally have information on copyright and moral rights for that country, and creators associations will offer advice in this area.

Your moral rights are:

- The right to be identified as the author (creator) of the work (right of paternity).

- The right to object to derogatory treatment of the work which could harm the reputation of the author (right of integrity in USA).

- The right not to have a work falsely attributed to you (called the right to object to false attribution in USA).

In the USA, moral rights only apply to original visual works produced for exhibition purposes, and are therefore of limited use to illustrators. They do not include the right of paternity. In the UK they are rights that exist for all creators, although the right of attribution has to be asserted – claimed in writing – before it applies. Unlike copyright, moral rights cannot be sold, but in the UK they can be waived (given up), and also do not apply to work in newspapers and magazines.

It's important for artists to be able to object to derogatory treatment of their work in order to protect their professional reputation.
Anna Steinberg

13 Anna Steinberg, 'Cyclists', an illustration selected for London Transport Museum's 'Year of Cycling' exhibition, 2010.

THE STAGES
OF FORMING A
CONTRACT

THE TERMS OF
AN AGREEMENT

WHO OWNS
THE RIGHTS?

Your ethics

Business runs more smoothly if participants behave in an appropriate, respectful manner to each other. This means:

- Delivering on the promise of your portfolio – producing work to the same standard as that which art directors have seen in your folio or website.

- Delivering visuals and final artwork to deadlines.

- Ensuring that clients understand which rights they are purchasing (illustrator and client have equal responsibility to make sure this happens).

- Being prepared to make minor alterations in artwork if required.

- Honouring an exclusivity clause – if you have given a client exclusive rights in a commissioned work that cannot be re-licensed during the licence period.

Most artists are influenced by those they admire during the time they are developing their own style, but consciously imitating the style of another artist is ethically unsound and unprofessional, even if requested by a client.

14 Tyra van Zweigbergk, 'Face', for *Tecknaren* magazine. An illustration demonstrating the importance of securing rights on how your work can be changed.

The right to be credited is important as it means that future clients know who created the image and can find you to commission you. It also helps you to build up a general reputation.
Tyra van Zweigbergk

THE IMPORTANCE OF BUSINESS SKILLS:
CAROLINE ATTIA LARIVIÈRE

Caroline Attia has been working as a freelance animation film director and illustrator since 2003. Her career involves directing animated films, art direction, design and animation on various projects and she also writes TV series, generates concepts and works as a graphic author. Running such a diverse business requires a strong set of business and organisational skills and she shares the load with her agents who manage about half of the work she produces: 'I am not represented in France anymore but work with several production houses here in France. In the US I have an illustration agent, Mendola Art, getting me a lot of work there.'

The work that she does is approached from two quite different directions. Most of her commercial work comes from commissions where she is approached directly or via her agents. At the same time she develops short films and TV series that are often speculative projects pitched directly to production companies. It's not unusual for her to be working on more than one series simultaneously; some aimed specifically at more commercial outcomes such as a pilot for a TV series, whilst others may have more personal or promotional objectives, such as pitching for the Annecy film competition.

Caroline describes the costing of the work that she does as 'the trickiest part of our job.' She reveals that she began learning about the financial dimension of the business only when she started gaining commissions. This she sees as an ongoing process of learning, achieved largely through visiting Internet forums and speaking with colleagues, as well as asking clients for advice.

She suggests that in the film and animation business, where there are various stages to consider, estimating the length of the project is an important aspect of this costing process: 'It's really necessary to know how much time you are going to take for each job and add a good amount of time for changes.' She reveals that the client can be supportive in the costing and reminds that it is always worthwhile to find out what the client is expecting to pay before suggesting a fee: 'I remember doing a three-minute film for an ad agency and they asked me to double my budget. I was amazed, but I ended up being happy!'

Balance between commissioned pieces and projects with less certain commercial outcomes is important for Caroline. Competitions and other personally initiated projects bring the potential for creative freedom and high-level exposure, often on an international stage, as well as bringing personal satisfaction: 'Sometimes I get so much commissioned work that I forget that I went into this media to tell stories. It's nice to get a good balance between commissioned and more personal projects.' She often applies for grants and sponsorship to subsidize these dimensions of her work, seeing that they are an investment for her business: 'Each part helps you get better at the other: commissions make you work faster under tight deadlines and create the processes to do so.'

1 Character design for the French TV series *Danny the Sneeze*, produced by Kawanimation.
2 Storyboard extract for a short film project, *ABC Kogis*.

1

2

CHAPTER SIX
FINANCE AND RUNNING A BUSINESS

At the beginning of a career, building up a client base and subsequently turning illustration into a profit-making enterprise is likely to take time. This period of attempting to break into the market can be disheartening for many freelancers. It may be difficult to sustain an interest and enthusiasm for developing a business if the returns are neither immediate nor plentiful. Being objective about your finances can help in assessing your prospects of surviving commercially, or to appraise the viability of your business over a longer term. Being successful financially means balancing the books, that is, ensuring that your incomings are greater than your outgoings.

Robert Sae-Heng

FREELANCE WORK
VS EMPLOYMENT

You always need to see yourself as a kind of small business. At first being a 'business' seems sort of an anathema to the idea of an 'artist', but really once you see yourself as a sole trader and artist in one, it allows you to respect your own work more and be more productive and creative, because suddenly your creative work is something that's just got to get done. And that helps your productivity. Approaching your creative work like a business – getting the boring stuff of promotion and book keeping and all that nailed – allows you to just get on with it and have a business-like attitude to your work. Business and creativity are two sides of one coin to an illustrator really.
Stephen Collins

Many illustrators decide to combine the early days of building a practice with part-time employment so that the pressure of surviving financially on a day-to-day basis is reduced. Committing yourself to the success of your business will inevitably need an injection of finance from other sources, and although for many illustrators at the early stages of a career financial reward is not the primary motivation, profiting from illustration is obviously an ultimate goal. Aiming to profit financially can be highly motivating.

Part-time work that is compatible or associated with illustration is obviously a perfect solution to sustainability. Combining design or arts administration, teaching, gallery work, employment in publishing or design-based retail can lead to illustration-relevant opportunities, but these areas are often highly competitive. Depending on your personal circumstances or individual flexibility, seasonal work or short-term contracts can provide an accumulation of funds which will be able to be filtered into your practice when you need them most. As deductions will be made automatically in most kinds of paid work, you don't need to take this into account when keeping accounts for your illustration practice, although if your tax entitlement is used up you will need to pay greater tax on any income from illustration work.

1

1 Stephen Collins, Death of a Hipster, cartoon for *The Guardian*.

FREELANCE WORK
VS EMPLOYMENT

MANAGING YOUR
BUSINESS

MANAGING YOUR
FINANCES

ADDITIONAL
SOURCES OF
INCOME

2

2 Jo Davies, 'Food Types',
illustration for *Understanding
Diabetes*, published by
Portsmouth Hospitals Trust.

**Working as a coach courier was
essentially a weekend job – I started
at 2pm Friday and finished at 2pm
Sunday. That was 48 hours non-stop
and 3,000 miles travel but I was
paid the equivalent of a full-time
job. It was exhausting and fun and
complemented my illustration practice
perfectly. Without the pressure of
wondering if I could pay the bills
I was able to spend a lot of time
developing my work and by the end
of the season I was getting regular,
well-paid freelance commissions.**
Jo Davies

EMPLOYED VS FREELANCE: LAURA HUGHES

'All my income comes from working as a freelance illustrator', says Laura Hughes. 'About 60% of my work comes from cards and licensing and 40% from children's books.' Of her income she reveals, 'It's a combination of royalties, advances and one-off payments.' In the early stages of Laura's career when work was slow in coming, taking a full-time job as a means of supporting freelance practice led to unforeseen gains: 'When I worked as a full-time manager for Paperchase my responsibilities included dealing with difficult customers, stock rotation and managing staff. That's all been really useful. When you work freelance and you're dealing with clients it's crucial that you are personable, able to work in a team and manage your time effectively.'

Through later work experience at the AOI and then working at Bright illustration agency, which now represents her, Laura gained a clearer understanding of the profession, becoming more adept at negotiating a route through it as an illustrator: 'I began to look at my own work more critically and became more commercial.' Financial success requires you to be business savvy, especially in the area of greetings cards, which can be low paid: 'I'm always conscious I need to license x amount of cards each month and books a year to earn a living. It's hard to gauge that on a month-to-month basis. As long as I have the work coming in I'm OK and as long as I'm owed money I know I have back-up.'

She is now conscious of what is commercially viable and how much to sell it for, mostly illustrating other authors' stories, creating commissioned pieces and licensing rights for wall canvasses, cards and stationery: 'I am strategic with how much time I put into a job compared to the fee, but you have to be realistic – it's a competitive climate. I put 100% into everything, even if it's on the low end of the pay scale.'

Being wise to the value of the time that she puts into all aspects of her business, and where to best invest this is vital: 'When you've not got a lot of time to spend on illustration, the ability to prioritize is key. Put your energy into fewer, but more important tasks. Always keep your end goals in mind and focus on what will lead to well-paid work.'

1

1 'Animals Christmas', a self-initiated illustration.
2 'Big Ben', work for The Almanac Gallery, London.

MANAGING YOUR BUSINESS

Keeping records

Managing the financial aspect of your business is a mandatory dimension of your illustration practice. Although you may be in a position to pay other professionals to handle some elements of it, you are responsible for understanding how your money is used and how to manage it to become financially stable.

Most freelancers have a flux in both their income and outgoings. Successful accounting entails projecting both expenditure and income over a long time span – usually a tax year – and making the income column at least match, but if possible exceed, the outgoings. To understand if your business is viable and make the most of the income you are generating, you will need to document and consider the pattern and nature of both your outgoings and your income. As you may be liable to pay tax and insurance based on income, keeping a clear record will be imperative in order to accurately complete your annual tax returns.

The outgoings of your business need to be covered to make a profit. Week-by-week or month-by-month, this can be difficult to assess, so projecting or forecasting expenditure against income over a longer period is necessary to take account of peaks and troughs. Setting realistic financial targets should be part of your plan. If you set up your business with a loan or injection of capital from some source or decide, as most freelancers do, to subsidize freelance practice by ongoing employment, you need to appraise the long-term viability of this, planning for the mid- and long-term future of your practice.

Below are some useful tips that may help when managing your business:

- Establish your main expenses each month and throughout the year and decide how you will cover these.

- Identify the point in the future at which you hope to be a self-sustaining freelancer.

- Calculate how many and what type of commissions you will need to cover your expenses.

- Identify any economies you can make by buying in bulk or in advance.

- Distinguish between what is essential to your practice and what is desirable.

- Keep records as you go along.

- Investigate the cost of paying a professional bookkeeper to organize your accounts and possibly submit any tax returns on your behalf.

FREELANCE WORK
VS EMPLOYMENT

**MANAGING
YOUR BUSINESS**

MANAGING YOUR
FINANCES

ADDITIONAL
SOURCES OF
INCOME

Some useful terms when working with the financial aspects of your practice are as follows:

- Accounts – you must produce an annual set of accounts and these are the summarized records of your business transactions.

- Balance sheet – a summary of the finances of a business, usually produced at the end of its financial year.

- Bookkeeping – the recording of financial transactions such as sales, purchases, income, receipts and payments.

- Income – money received for work carried out.

- Cash flow – expenses/outgoings and income flowing through your business over a certain time period.

- Invoice – the document that records the amount due in payment for an assignment.

- Outgoings – the sums you pay out in the running of your business.

- Profit – the amount you have left after all your expenditure.

- Loss – when expenses exceed income, resulting in a loss rather than a profit.

- Tax – duty to be paid to the government on income. Sales tax may be due in the USA.

- Tax entitlement – the amount you are allowed to earn before tax is due.

It's difficult when you're just embarking on a career as an illustrator to see the sense in spending money on self-promotion when you're struggling to keep your bank manager happy, and the admin side of setting yourself up can seem daunting. It definitely helps to talk to people already in the business and take note of their experiences. Regular bookkeeping and sorting out your accounts and tax can actually become quite satisfying and it gets easier as your career develops (really!). Initial financial outlay on promotion, such as mail-outs and keeping up a good website, will soon be recouped if it's directed to the right people. Get your work out there and make sure it stays out there!

Tom Jay

3 Tom Jay, an illustration for an article arguing for the reintroduction of the grammar school system in the UK, published in Saturday opinion page, *The Independent*.

Rates

Generally, you will be working out your fees for illustration commissions based on the use of the artwork, the geographical territory it will be used in and the duration of the licence agreed between you and your client. There are circumstances when this will not be the only way of pricing work undertaken for a commission, and that will be when you may apply a day or hourly rate.

A day rate will not be inclusive of the licence aspect of a commission – this usage of the artwork should always be negotiated separately from any work being priced on a time basis. These are some examples of when a time-based rate would apply:

- Additional time spent on existing artwork, over and above agreed revisions.

- Devising artwork which is then to be applied to many different areas or products on a licence basis, known as an artwork origination fee.

- Paid pitching for a potential commission (for example, if you are asked by a design company to create artwork for a pitch they are making to a potential client).

A day or hourly rate should take into account your studio costs (rent, electricity, heating), travel to studio if away from your home, any materials used and any other expenses you incur. A guideline at the time of writing would be around £25–30 ($40–50) per hour, £250–300 ($400–500) per day.

Desk space in a shared studio is likely to be the biggest single expense in an illustrator's financial year, but it can prove to be one of the most worthwhile in terms of creative atmosphere; sharing ideas and bouncing them off the other studio members; feeling part of a creative community rather than isolated at home; having a useable workspace that isn't too much of a compromise and getting some balance and discipline regarding work time/place that a dedicated space can give to your working day.
Robin Heighway-Bury

4 Robin Heighway-Bury, 'Egg Man', promotional work.

FREELANCE WORK
VS EMPLOYMENT

**MANAGING
YOUR BUSINESS**

MANAGING YOUR
FINANCES

ADDITIONAL
SOURCES OF
INCOME

I work out my costs based on:

- **The number of days it will take me to make (prep time).**
- **The number of days it will take to photograph (I usually get a photographer to quote for their part including their studio equipment hire, etc.).**
- **How much assistance I need.**
- **Cost of materials (I always overestimate on material costs in case I need to make changes).**
- **Usage, if applicable.**
- **Contingency – I allow flexibility with my day rate so there's room for negotiation with the client.**

Hattie Newman

5 Hattie Newman, 'Lollies', promotional materials. Models of ice lollies were wrapped, sealed and sent out to clients with a postcard.

Covering the costs of your business

You may occasionally come across the attitude that as you are working in a creative industry, just the pleasure of making artwork should be reward enough, and a decent fee is not required for your services. However, you are running a freelance business, and it is important to acknowledge that fact. You are offering an individual service providing unique work of value, and providing that service is an expense to you in time, place of work, materials, hardware and software, use of the telephone and the Internet.

Some of the outgoing costs that you will incur are as follows:

- Studio rent (whether a space in your home, or specific studio).

- Telephone and broadband (land-line rental, mobile/cell pay-as-you-go, or monthly package).

- Promotion and marketing (including Internet: website hosting and domain name).

- Stationery.

- Insurance (this will include health insurance in USA).

- Business bank account charges.

- Travel.

- Postage.

Registering with the tax office

You will be required to register with the tax office once starting to work as a freelancer, to keep records of your business and pay tax once your earnings reach a limit set by the tax office. Your country's government website will direct you to information on setting up a small business and when and how you need to pay tax and other contributions.

National Insurance contributions are payable in the UK by the self-employed when earnings reach a certain level. UK residents are sent a National Insurance number before their sixteenth birthday.

In the USA, freelancers are required to obtain a licence to conduct business from some cities and states; to register a business name if not using your own full name and obtain a state tax ID.

6

FREELANCE WORK
VS EMPLOYMENT

**MANAGING
YOUR BUSINESS**

MANAGING YOUR
FINANCES

ADDITIONAL
SOURCES OF
INCOME

Working for free

Being eager to have work commissioned and published within the public domain can make accepting illustration work for free, or for a token payment, an appealing prospect. Providing a professional service merits a professional payment, by working for free you are undermining the value of what illustration professionals do, as well as your own value. If the client cannot offer a fee for work, try to negotiate other value from the commission. Ask them to extend the print run, for example, and take more samples in lieu of payment, which could provide you a valuable source of promotion.

Other forms of payment could include a share of future profits (similar to royalties) or payment in kind. If you do work for free, ensure you operate in the same way as you would for paid work – be clear about your rights in writing, and in particular identify any claim to future profits. The band your friend is in may become an international success and your unpaid CD cover or poster may contribute to that.

As an up-and-coming illustrator, I've worked at a low rate and even for free. A few jobs that I've done just for fun for friends have led on to bringing in great press, which later generated paid work from clients.
Sophia Chang

6 Sophia Chang, 'Coming to America', self-generated work.

MANAGING YOUR FINANCES   Payment

Running your own freelance business means that you are required to maintain accurate records of income, expenditure and expenses. These will be needed to supply to the tax office to ascertain your tax payments.

It is advisable not to operate your business through a personal bank account – keep your business finance clearly separate from your personal to avoid any possible confusion. Research the business bank account that suits you best and open it in time for your first income and outgoings. There is generally a monthly fee for business bank accounts, which you can claim as a business expense.

It is also recommended to open a separate savings account to regularly deposit sums that will be necessary for tax purposes. Many freelancers have been caught short when faced with a tax bill – it is better to be prepared.

You will not automatically receive payment for work that you do as a freelancer. It is common practice to issue an invoice which outlines what pay you are claiming and in relation to which commission. This will usually be handled by the accounts department of whichever company you have worked for, even if you submit it via the art director who was your direct line of contact. It is advisable that you follow the standard format for invoices – they need to be functional and clear so that payment can be met efficiently. (See Appendix, page 181) The internal accounting processes of each company differ – some will need to set up a system to pay directly into your bank account, others will pay by cheque. As it is usual for payments to be met on specific calendar dates, your payment may not be within a time frame that makes direct sense to your own.

If payment has not been made within six weeks to two months, you may need to query this directly with the accounts department. Don't think that pressing for payment may jeopardize your chances of further work with the company. You are entitled to payment for work you have undertaken. It's likely that whoever commissioned you will be sympathetic and may be able to assist you by liaising with their accounts department if payments are exceptionally delayed.

7 Zachariah OHora, spread from his picture book *Stop Snoring, Bernard!* published by Henry Holt. The book was a winner of the 2011 Society of Illustrator's Founders Award and the PA One Book for 2012.

7

In publishing I always work to royalty agreements. Most houses have a standard percentage. Sometimes there's some wiggle room, but an escalation clause is one of the ways you can get a little bit more. Basically it says if you sell X amount of books, anything after that number has a higher royalty rate. And it's usually a number that the publisher is comfortable with, in that, if you hit it in sales, they've well covered their costs already.
Zachariah OHora

FREELANCE WORK
VS EMPLOYMENT

MANAGING YOUR
BUSINESS

**MANAGING YOUR
FINANCES**

ADDITIONAL
SOURCES OF
INCOME

Royalties and flat fees

Many illustration commissions are remunerated by a single payment for the use of the artwork. Others, such as interior book illustrations and merchandising items, may receive royalty payments over the period of time the product is available for.

Royalties are commonly applied to books, whether physical or digital, apps, merchandising items, giftware, (greetings cards, toys, calendars), and are payments to the illustrator based on a percentage of the money generated by the quantity of items that are sold. For example, a book illustrator would receive a percentage of the sums collected by the publisher on sales of a title.

It is usual for royalties to be paid in installments over the period of time that the product is available for sale, so greetings card royalty payments may be made by the producer four times per year whereas a book royalty is paid twice per year.

Advances

It is possible to receive an advance on royalties, which is a payment made before the commissioned work is available for sale and this advance is generally a lump sum. Once royalty payments have accrued from sales to cover the advance payment, royalties will become due.

Occasionally, a client may offer either a one-off fee or royalty earnings (with or without an advance). Accepting royalties can be a gamble, as there can be no guarantee that the product will sell enough to earn any substantial royalties.

Illustration is applied to many retail and merchandising products, such as cards, toys, stationery and T-shirts. If you are commissioned to create images for these items you can expect to be offered a percentage on either the producer's gross receipts/ recommended retail price, or on the producer's net receipts (see Appendix, page 176). Royalties are generally offered at 5–10% of these receipts. As a rough guide, net receipts translate to about 50% of gross receipts, so it is preferable to negotiate royalties on gross if possible.

Understanding finance is very important for all freelancers, of any field. Unfortunately I did not learn about finances as an illustrator until after my first year of taxes. It is important to keep track of your expenses and pay close attention to your budget. I now keep organized monthly files that show my income and expenses.
Sophia Chang

We generally offer royalties if we are publishing a collection of work, usually a minimum of 12 designs by one artist. This route means that artists receive a percentage of each card sold. Often they can request a small advance against royalties that they have to earn in sales before receiving any royalty payments. The royalty calculation is based on net sales and also allows for a percentage of returns for unsold cards. Royalties can be far more rewarding if the designs sell well over a long period of time, but they are more of a gamble; if the designs do not sell, the royalty returns will be lower and in fact may not reach the flat fee level.
Nick Adsett,
Great British Card Company

8

8 Victoria Hooper-Duckham, card design for the Great British Card Company.

ADDITIONAL SOURCES OF INCOME

Once your artwork has been published, you may be in a position to claim from additional sources of income for creators. This can be in the form of fees paid for book library loans or under an extended collective licensing scheme. Registering for these schemes is recommended, as even insubstantial payments can be welcome.

Collective licensing

Collective licensing is used for secondary licensing in the UK and European countries in situations where it would be difficult for artists and authors to license the rights they hold in published works, such as books and magazines, on an individual basis. All rights holders are opted into the collective licensing, and it is organized through collective management societies such as:

DACS Payback scheme: www.dacs.org.uk

European Visual Artists (EVA): www.evartists.org

Public lending right (PLR)

Artists whose work is published in books may be able to claim for library loan payments. In the UK, Public Lending Right (PLR) legislation forms the right for contributors to books to receive payment for loans of their books from public libraries. To be eligible, the artist's name needs to be on the title page of the book, or they are entitled to a royalty payment from the book publisher. Titles have to be registered with PLR (www.plr.uk.com) to be part of the scheme (see Appendix, page 180).

Many other countries have public lending schemes, including Canada, who compensate for the free public access to books in public libraries, although the USA does not. For information on current international lending schemes go to www. plrinternational.com.

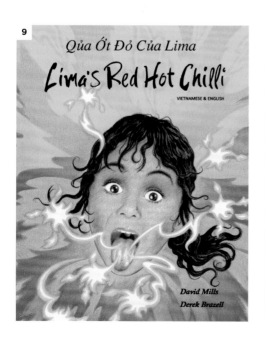

9 Derek Brazell, book cover for the digital edition of *Lima's Red Hot Chilli*, published by Mantra.

10 David Roberts, book cover for the children's book *Pooh! is that You, Bertie?*, published by Little Tiger Press.

FREELANCE WORK
VS EMPLOYMENT

MANAGING YOUR
BUSINESS

MANAGING YOUR
FINANCES

**ADDITIONAL
SOURCES OF
INCOME**

11

Payback gives Illustrators a sense of worth in their work, both monetary and ethically. The intellectual property of an artwork is an illustrator's greatest asset and by applying for Payback, you are not only receiving a sum of money but also strengthening the sense of the value of your copyright and its use by others.

It's also very considerate the time of year that the payments are made. For what is a short time spent filling out a form; Payback literally saved Christmas for me last year and made sure that both my nieces received decent presents!

Paul Ryding

11 Paul Ryding, 'Ulla', self-generated piece.

Editioning

If there is an authorial dimension to your practice and you make zines, prints, books, toys or other artefacts that include imagery, it may be that you could consider editioning as you set a value for the pieces you plan to sell. In making a limited edition you are creating a pre-determined batch of items and clearly numbering each accordingly. A limited edition is normally hand signed and numbered by the artist, typically in pencil. For example, with 20/100, the first number is the number of the piece and the second number is the number of pieces that will be issued overall. There can be an implied worth in the rarity value of smaller editions. The lower the second number is, the more valuable and collectible the limited editions are likely to be. If you are making work through traditional print techniques, such as screen prints, linocut or etching, editioning may be a familiar option. Giclée prints are the contemporary means of creating digital editions.

12 Adolie Day, editioned prints.

FREELANCE WORK
VS EMPLOYMENT

MANAGING YOUR
BUSINESS

MANAGING YOUR
FINANCES

**ADDITIONAL
SOURCES OF
INCOME**

13

13 Michael Kirkham, limited
edition print.

3/200

Michael Kirkham 2012.

ACTIVITIES

ACTIVITY 1
Where to work

ACTIVITY 2
Skills audit

ACTIVITY 3
Reflecting your potential in your portfolio

ACTIVITY 4
Contacting potential clients

ACTIVITY 5
Promotional strategy

ACTIVITY 6
Understanding fees

ACTIVITY 7
Costing

WHERE TO WORK

AIMS

- Identify some of the defining features and possible strengths of your work
- Identify areas which you aspire towards

Opposite, compiled from various agents and portfolio websites, is a composite list of some of the descriptors of illustration currently being promoted. Some of these are style or media based, some of them are technical descriptors and others refer to the genre or subject. You may be able to add categories of your own.

The third column lists the areas that illustrators work in. Many artists can fit within several of these headings and they aren't mutually exclusive.

Tick all the descriptors which relate to your work.

Ring the areas which you think your work could be commissioned for. It's likely that there will be more than one.

2D digital

3D rendering

Abstract

Animation animals and nature

Architectural

Art deco

Automobiles

Boutique

Business

Beauty

Calligraphy

Caricature

Cartoon

Characters

Character development

Children's illustration

Comic books

Collage

Concept art

Cutaway art

Decorative

Digital

Diagrams

Fantasy

Fashion

Food and drink

Graffiti

Graphic imagery

Graphic novels

Icons

Infographics

Interactive

Landscapes

Lettering

Licensing

Maps

Medical

Motion

Mural design

Narrative based

Natural history

Naive

Oil /acrylic

Painterly

Paper sculpture

Pen and ink

Photo illustration/montage

Prints

Portraits

Realistic

Satirical

Sci-Fi

Silhouettes

Site-based work

Storyboards

Surface pattern

Surrealism

Technical

Textiles

Toy design

Traditional

Transport

Typography

Vintage

Watercolour

Editorial

Publishing

Illustration for screen

Concept artists

Games design

Decorative

Reportage

Authorial

Design

SKILLS AUDIT

AIMS

- **Evaluate your strengths**
- **Recognize areas for development**
- **Produce an action plan**
- **Establish achievable short, medium and long-term goals**

PART A
GENERIC SKILLS AUDIT

To work in an identifiable visual language

To be stylistically consistent

To use colour

To work in black and white

To read and understand a brief

To generate and select a range of ideas for a client

To visualize ideas for a client

To locate and appropriately use visual research when required

To work across a broad range of subject areas

To make corrections to an image

To undertake personal work

To create authorial work

To create promotional work

Technical skills

To work in given formats

To scan a piece of artwork

To prepare artwork digitally

To save artwork in the appropriate format and colour mode

To order printed work

To set up and add content to a blog or website

To access the web

To communicate via email

Transferable skills

To communicate clearly in written and verbal forms

To organize time

To work to a deadline

To work quickly if required

To manage resources

To work independently

To work in a team

To adapt to change

To respond to criticism

Business skills

To communicate with clients

To understand the commissioning process

To take a brief

To organize a contract/licence

To work out a fee

To negotiate terms

To issue an invoice

To be self-supporting financially

To manage finances

Evaluate yourself according to these skills on a scale of 1–5 with 5 being your strongest. Refer to the areas that you identified earlier to see if your own skills match those required.

These lists of skills are neither finite, nor exhaustive and you may wish to add to them.

PART B
SPECIALIST SKILLS AUDIT

PUBLISHING

Working for children, including text books
Ability to create a diversity of characters and convincing environments

Ability to depict various racial types

Ability to use characters consistently

Ability to depict expressions and moods

Ability to interpret a text

Stylistic consistency

Understanding of sequence and pacing

Ability to make a dummy book

Confidence in positioning text

Writing ability

Working to tight deadlines

Awareness of the requirements of co-editions with different countries

Comic books
Developing and sustaining storyline over many pages and spreads

Understanding how to structure a book

Creating a dummy book

Understanding the function of text and images

Consistency of character

Independent publishing
Constructing books

Creating and working with narrative

Understanding how to produce limited editions

Book jackets
Ability to interpret narrative

Understanding of composition in relation to text space requirements

Use of hand-rendered text for titles

EDITORIAL ILLUSTRATION
Ability to work quickly

Ability to explore and visualize ideas

Ability to work with diverse subjects

DESIGN, INCLUDING NON-PRINT-BASED DESIGN

Illustration for screen, including Web and moving image (dependent on the role you hope to achieve)

Skills in relevant software

Idea generation

Character development

Ability to visualize ideas

Ability to storyboard

Ability to draw diverse subjects

Ability to work quickly

Ability to work in a team

Concept art

Up-to-date knowledge of computer illustration software packages

Conversant with film imagery

Good understanding of what directors, directors of photography and editors require from a scene

Ability to visualize perspective and 3D space

Modelling skills

Knowledge of design, architecture and film

Ability to visually interpret other people's ideas

Decorative including 3D objects, toys, surface and site-based work

Awareness of current trends

Ability to create a range of connected ideas

Ability to generate ideas autonomously

Understanding of specialist processes, techniques and technical issues relevant to the product

Reportage

Ability to work from reference

Ability to work in a variety of situations

Ability to work under pressure

Ability to connect socially and network

Authorial

Understanding how to produce limited editions

Marketing ability

Appropriate craft skills

Advertising

Ability to work closely with an art director

Ability to visualize clearly

Ability to work under pressure

Willingness to be adaptable

PART C
ACTION PLAN

Make a list of the skills that you have scored lowly. (If you have only top scores, it may be that you are reading this book for recreational purposes only!)

This list can become the basis for an action plan simply by adding 'Action' and 'By when' to each skill.

When answering 'Action', you should include immediate practical factors, like resources available to you.

You could organize them into order of priority deciding upon which, if any, will have most direct influence or benefit to your current work situation.

EXAMPLES

AIM 1
■ **To work across a broad range of subject areas**

Action:
Do some self-initiated briefs suitable for a children's publication and also look at mocking up some existing work into other contexts, using Photoshop, and send these out as PDFs to possible clients.

By when:
Ongoing, but aim to send new work out in a promotional PDF to first list of potential clients within six weeks' time.

AIM 2
■ **Finding possible clients**

Action:
Visit a local newsagent and take contact details for any new magazines. Look at other illustrators' client lists to see who they have been working for. Look at the design press to see which companies are featured and which companies are using illustration.

By when:
Make a trip to the newsagent's to coincide with your next shopping trip to large stores.
Begin looking immediately for other illustrators online. Do this for 30 minutes each day until a list of 40 new possible clients is established.

REFLECTING YOUR POTENTIAL IN YOUR PORTFOLIO

AIMS

■ **To consider possible avenues for your work and to ensure that your folio reflects your potential to operate within these genres**

a. Make a list of the generic areas that you hope to work in.

b. Make an additional list of all possible client types within each generic area.

c. Make a list of all the formats and applications that exist within these areas.

d. Look objectively at your folio – does it demonstrate that you are capable of working in these areas?

e. Create an action plan to either mock up some existing work within suitable formats to demonstrate its potential application within a selected range of applications within this genre, or aim to undertake some sample briefs.

EXAMPLE

Generic area
Children's work

Possible clients
Publishing, surface and decorative, children's services (playgroups, nurseries, kids' party organizers, child-minding services, kids' activity clubs, kids' theatre), fashion, children's retailers (toyshops, cafés, clothes, educational, etc.).

Possible formats and applications
Posters, logos, playpacks, packaging, retail design, murals, educational materials, animations, books, magazines, textiles, stationery, greetings cards, clothing, toys, character design, interiors, apps, etc.

To produce convincing mock-ups, you need to understand:

How imagery is commissioned. What its function is in relation to its format and intended audience. How imagery works within its context, e.g. how it relates to the text in an editorial context. The scale and 3D properties of a package, The functionality of a space if it is a site-based piece. How it communicates.

LIST

Generic area

Possible clients

Possible formats and applications

Generic area

Possible clients

Possible formats and applications

Generic area

Possible clients

Possible formats and applications

Generic area

Possible clients

Possible formats and applications

CONTACTING POTENTIAL CLIENTS

As your reputation grows and you become more established your potential clients will find you. At the early stages of your career, however, your aim should be to locate potential clients and make them aware of what you are offering.

LIST

Details:

Details:

Company name:

Company name:

Address:

Address:

Tel.:
Email:

Tel.:
Email:

Company name:

Company name:

Address:

Address:

Tel.:
Email:

Tel.:
Email:

Company name:

Company name:

Address:

Address:

Tel.:
Email:

Tel.:
Email:

AIM

■ **To create a database of useful contact details for potential clients**

a. Collect details for the companies you aspire to get work from. Aim to be as broad and inclusive as possible – include international brands as well as local companies.

b. Begin to add individuals' names, contact emails and addresses. You may have to be a detective to find these. Some pointers:

- Search on artists' blogs
- Search on company websites
- Search on folio sites
- Search on subject association sites
- Ring other artists
- Ring the companies directly
- Search any available current listings books
- Search local directories
- Search local magazines and newspapers

NB: Don't take for granted that details you find or are given are accurate – ring through to switchboards of major companies and check.

Aim to get hundreds of names and numbers. If 10% of one hundred potential clients you mail are positive, and one rings with a commission, you may have enough for this week's rent... what about next week's rent?

PROMOTIONAL STRATEGY

AIM 1

■ **To create a long-term promotional strategy**

Part 1
Customize each item on the list you made for Activity 3 to make each heading relate to your own ambitions and type of work. There may be more than one entry next to each item. Don't censor what you write because they are currently outside of your financial means.
E.g. Next to 'postcard' write the titles of the images which best represent your work. Next to 'artefact' write as many things which could be created as a vehicle for your own imagery – typical artefacts can be badges, bookmarks, canvas bags, cut-outs, etc. Research to find the names of the paid folio sites which include your type of work.

Make a list of dates for key competitions and trade fairs, in your home country and abroad.

Part 2
Group what you have listed as potential forms of self-promotion according to each of the categories 'essential', 'desirable' and 'highly desirable' in terms of where you are in your career at this time.

AIM 2

■ To cost out the implementation of a promotional campaign

Beginning with your list of essential categories, do a costing of what your outlay would be to create each of the separate items on the list. With each you want to consider doing it yourself as well as the alternative option of paying (or bartering) with someone externally.

It's usual when getting quotes externally, such as from printers of postcards, to consider several options.

With printing, consider the benefits of buying in larger quantities but only if you are sure that the image you select is sufficiently representative of what you do and of broad enough interest. A bigger print run is only good economy if you have a large distribution list: your image is likely to quickly become dated and leftover promotional materials will soon become obsolete. When costing out making printed samples or making limited editions or artefacts, factor in all the materials you will need, even if you have them already – printing ink, paper, scalpels, spray glue, etc.

Factor in your time. If you are supporting yourself with a part-time job, it may be cheaper to work more hours and pay for the work to be done externally.

Include the cost of envelopes, packaging and postage.

With a stand at a trade fair or stall, cost how much it would be to share this with other illustrator friends.

UNDERSTANDING FEES

AIM

■ **To gain an understanding of fee structures**

Listed opposite are several commissions. Organize the list according to what you believe would be the highest fee. Take into account all the factors which will influence this decision. If you are able to, research actual fees for similar jobs. This may help you create an accurate, simple fee structure that could be useful in considering future commissions of your own.

Make a list of applications of illustration that you encounter such as advertising, packaging, editorials, decorative products, illustration used in publishing, and get into the habit of estimating what terms you would expect if you were the illustrator commissioned to produce the image and what fee you would have expected to be reasonable.

Book jacket for international bestseller
- Publisher – international
- Rights – world rights, volume (paper) and digital rights
- Duration – four years
- Secondary uses – to be used for large-scale promotional point-of-sale campaign in bookstores.

Book jacket for independent publisher
- Print run 500
- Duration – two years
- UK distribution

Cover and five B/W spot illustrations for major finance company
- For company brochure distributed internally
- Print run 5,000
- Duration – one year
- International distribution

Cover and five B/W spot illustrations for major finance company
- For company brochure distributed as part of major advertising campaign
- Below-the-line direct mail
- Print run 20,000
- Duration – one year
- International distribution

COSTING

AIM

■ **To create a projection of your financial expenditure over the first year of your freelance business**

You will need to draw a grid with each month of a 12-month period as headings across the top – begin with the month that you launch your business.

Under each month list your domestic expenditure (i.e. what you spend to live).

As an example this may include all or some of these listed personal outgoings – you may have others depending on your individual circumstances. Put a realistic figure against each column to establish a monthly total. And add this total under each month.

Do the same for your annual expenditure – here you are including the irregular costs such as medicine, insurance, gifts, holidays, etc., which may be one-off or fluctuating outgoings. Some of these figures will be estimates but you can set the ceiling – the most you expect to spend. For columns such as promotion in the business section you may break this down into subsections – the cost of printed samples, website design, buying an actual folio, and these may vary from year to year. Although you may already have all the equipment you need, it will eventually need updating or replacing and the cost of this should be factored in. Put these figures under the appropriate months so that you can easily evaluate where there is heavy or light expenditure.

PERSONAL

Monthly regular outgoings
- Rent
- Utilities
- Monthly consumerables – food, socializing, phone, entertainment

One-off payments or irregular outgoings
- Clothes
- Gifts
- Holidays
- Insurance policies
- Dental and medical

BUSINESS

Monthly
- Phone
- Internet

Annual or irregular outgoings
- Promotion
- Travel
- Materials
- Equipment
- Membership to trade organizations
- Subscriptions to magazines
- Exhibition costs
- Post/packaging
- Entering competitions
- Visiting trade shows

Against each month total add the expected expenditure to get a figure which will be the sum of your annual outgoings. Divide the final expenditure or outgoings across 12 months so that you are distributing the burden equally, irrespective of how it actually falls on the calendar.

This is the figure you need to earn monthly to survive entirely from your illustration practice.

ASK YOURSELF SOME QUESTIONS

- How many jobs will you need over the year to realize the monthly/yearly expenditure?
- How will you deal with cash flow crisis?
- Which are the most demanding months and how will you deal with these?
- Can you project this annual forecast within the context of a longer term plan?
- Will the income from your illustration business supplement your main income?
- What is the time scale in which you aim for illustration to become the main source of your income?
- What do you need to do with promotion/ revising your folio to become potentially more commercial?

EXERCISE

AIM

■ **To create actual accounts for a specified time period**

Collect all the receipts that you have actually generated for your business within a given month.

Use these headings to itemize your actual expenditure (outgoings) and earnings (income).

OUTGOINGS

- Premises (including share of business-related utilities)
- Promotion
- Communication
- Materials/equipment/resources
- Competitions
- Memberships
- Travel
- Insurance contributions

Add together to get the total of your outgoings for the month.

Make a second list of the income for the month. This should be the totals from the invoices you have issued, whether you have already received payment or not, and any artwork sold. Only include income from freelance work – NOT income from employment.

Deduct the outgoings from the income. If the figure is a minus number, that will be a loss figure for the month. If it's a positive, that will be a profit. Carry this figure forward to the next month so that you can keep a running total of loss or profit.

APPENDIX

- **TECHNICAL TIPS**
- **A GUIDE TO LICENSING**
- **CONTRACT SAMPLES**
- **SAMPLE TERMS AND CONDITIONS**
- **A GUIDE TO FINANCE**
- **A SAMPLE INVOICE**
- **USEFUL RESOURCES**
- **IMAGE CREDITS**
- **INDEX**
- **ACKNOWLEDGEMENTS**

TECHNICAL TIPS

Files

Most clients ask for artwork to be supplied digitally and the conventions are standard and should be followed.

Size

If created in Photoshop or equivalent, it should be at least 300 dpi for print quality. If an original is scanned at print size, the same applies but if the final print version will be larger than the original, it must be scanned at a higher resolution to allow for the increase in scale. Specific technical information to achieve this is available from various online sources. Photoshop images will take up more memory if layers have not been flattened. If delivered to the client in this format, layers could be adapted without your permission.

If images are required for digital use, including your own website, they will not need to be saved at print quality. Digital use only requires that images be saved at 72 dpi, and choosing the 'Save for Web' option in your program significantly reduces the file size. High res. images can be more easily appropriated for unauthorized print use. Low res. files will load quickly and allow your images to be seen rapidly on screen giving a more client-friendly interface.

Mode

It's important to note that colour files should be created in one of two modes for print and digital use.

CMYK mode (Cyan, Magenta, Yellow, Black) must be used for print as these are the colours of the inks used in the printing process. RGB mode (Red, Green, Blue) is the colour of light emitted by screens and therefore used for digital artwork.

Digital artwork delivery

There are various ways to deliver digital files to a client. If the client has agreed to receive work by email it can be sent as an attachment. This is only suitable for smaller files. Using online delivery services or file-sharing systems will guarantee a file will arrive and maintain quality.

Research online for big file transfer options.

Original physical artwork

If you have agreed to supply artwork in a physical format to be scanned by the client, ensure your name and contact details are clearly visible on the back of each piece and cover with protective material. As the artwork remains your property remember to agree a date by which artwork should be returned.

Crop marks and bleed

Crop marks define the edges of your image and indicate where a page will be cut (or trimmed) after printing. A bleed is needed for artwork which extends to the edge of a printed page. By continuing your image beyond the crop mark for at least 0.5cm (0.19in) on the edges to be cropped, possible errors in trimming will be minimized.

If your artwork includes text elements, check with your client if these need to be provided as a separate layer from the image. This is needed in picture books, for example, if text will need to be translated for foreign publication.

Archiving

Keeping records and copies of each commission will be useful for your own ongoing business and practice. It is essential to back up all artwork on external storage for future reference. The commissioner may require future re-use of an image.

A GUIDE TO LICENSING

Some common terms

All media rights: This is a licence term which allows the client to use the artwork in all media (digital, print, multimedia, broadcast, etc.).

Exclusive use: This right means that only the purchaser of these rights may reproduce the artwork.

Contract: An agreement between two parties (e.g. illustrator and client) where they agree to perform certain obligations.

Purchase order: Form from client to illustrator which details the elements of the commission. This should be given before work commences.

Net receipts: Income received by producer once all expenses and taxes have been deducted. Sometimes called wholesale price.

Gross receipts: Sum received from sale of an item before expenses are deducted.

Royalty: A payment calculated on a percentage of income from number of items sold which is given to the artist. Royalties may be offered on books, apps, cards and merchandising items.

Work-for-hire (USA only): This term may appear as part of a contract and means that the commissioner will be the owner of the copyright, rather than the creator. It should be resisted.

Copyright

Copyright allows for the exclusive legal right to reproduce, sell and publish your work, and comes into being as soon as a work is created. Registration of your artwork is not required for copyright protection to apply.

In the USA formal registration of work with the U.S. Copyright Office of the Library of Congress offers additional benefits in the form of proof of authorship in the work, evidence of copyright ownership should it be required by a court, and the option to recover statutory damages (awarded by the court) for a copyright infringement. There are certain time periods by which the creative works must be registered for the benefits to be effective. Form VA is required for registration.

USA Copyright Office:

- www.copyright.gov/circs/circ01.pdf
- www.copyright.gov/circs/index.html#f

Moral rights

- UK: Right of paternity: The right to be identified as the author.
- Right of integrity: right not to have the work subjected to derogatory treatment.
- Right not to have authorship of works falsely attributed to one.
- USA: Personal creators' rights in original works, irrespective of sale of work or assignment of copyright in it. Do not apply to reproduce works.
- USA: Visual Artists Rights Act of 1990 (VARA).

Examples of licensed artwork

Greetings Cards

- Usage – x number of illustrations and where they would be used, e.g. boxed set, stand alone, mixed pack, etc.
- Duration – usually one or two years.
- Territory – could be worldwide or specific country.
- Fee – either flat fee or royalties.

Advertising Poster

- Usage – size and location e.g., 48-sheet billboard, four-sheet transit/bus shelter.
- Duration – maybe short time period, e.g. six months.
- Territory – local, national or global.
- Fee – usually a flat fee. Secondary uses, if relevant, will attract an additional fee. Profile of client will influence scale of fee.

Packaging

- Usage – type of client, type of product, scale of image e.g. front of packaging.
- Duration – varies, generally more than one year.
- Territory - local, national or global.
- Fee – usually a flat fee. Profile of client will influence scale of fee.

App

- Usage – commercial (for purchase or free) or internal corporate.
- Duration – varies.
- Territory – national or global.
- Fee - either flat fee or royalties.

CONTRACT SAMPLES

Contract

An acceptance of commission form should be supplied to your client for each commission should you not receive an equivalent. The text supplied here should be sufficient for most commissions. However, note that in particular, picture book contracts, which will be supplied by the publisher, involve additional clauses relating to royalties, co-edition agreements and subsidiary rights, such as translation and merchandising rights.

ACCEPTANCE OF COMMISSION

- To:
- For your commission for artwork as follows:
- Title/Subject:
- Commissioned by:
- Delivery dates:
- Roughs:
- Artwork:
- Fee: £/$
- Expenses: £/$

TERMS OF LICENCE TO BE GRANTED

- Customer:
- Use:
- Area covered by licence:
- Duration:
- Exclusive/non-exclusive:
- Credits
- A credit for non-editorial work? (see Clause 23)
- Special terms (if any):

The Standard Terms and Conditions for this commission and for the later licensing of any rights are included here. Please review them together with the above and let me know immediately if you have any objection or queries. Otherwise it will be understood that you have accepted them.

THIS COMMISSION IS SUBJECT TO ALL THE FOLLOWING TERMS AND CONDITIONS

- Signature of Illustrator:
- Date:

SAMPLE TERMS AND CONDITIONS

Ownership of Copyright/ Copyright Licence

1. The copyright in artwork commissioned by the Client shall be retained by the Illustrator.

2. The Client or the Client's customer (where the Client is acting as an intermediary) is granted a licence to reproduce the artwork solely for the purposes set out on the face of this acceptance of commission. If the acceptance of commission is silent, the Client or the Client's customer is granted an exclusive licence for one time use in the United Kingdom only.

3. During the currency of the licence the Illustrator shall notify the Client of any proposed exploitation of the artwork for purposes other than self-promotion and the Client shall have the right to make reasonable objections if such exploitation is likely to be detrimental to the business of the Client or the Client's customer.

4. Where use of the artwork is restricted, the Illustrator will nominally grant the Client or the Client's customer a licence for use for other purposes subject to payment of a further fee in line with current licensing rates to be mutually agreed between the Illustrator and Client.

5. The licence hereby granted to use the artwork is contingent upon the Illustrator having received payment in full of all monies due to her/him and no reproduction or publication rights are granted unless and until all sums due under this Agreement have been paid.

6. The licence hereby granted is personal to the Client or the Client's customer (where the Client is acting as an intermediary) and the rights may not be assigned or sub-licensed to third parties without the Illustrator's consent.

Payment

7. The Client shall pay all invoices within 30 days of their receipt.

Cancellation

8. If a commission is cancelled by the Client, the Client shall pay a cancellation fee as follows:

i. 25% of the agreed fee if the commission is cancelled before delivery of roughs;

ii. 33% of the agreed fee if the commission is cancelled at the rough stage;

iii. 100% of the agreed fee if the commission is cancelled on the delivery of artwork;

iv. pro rata if the commission is cancelled at an intermediate stage.

9. In the event of cancellation, ownership of all rights granted under this Agreement shall revert to the Illustrator unless the artwork is based on the Client's visual or otherwise agreed.

Delivery

10. The Illustrator shall use her/his best endeavours to deliver the artwork to the Client by the agreed date and shall notify the Client of any anticipated delay at the first opportunity in which case the Client may (unless the delay is the fault of the Client) make time of the essence and cancel the commission without payment in the event of the Illustrator failing to meet the agreed date.

11. The Illustrator shall not be liable for any consequential loss or damage arising from late delivery of the artwork.

12. The Client shall make an immediate objection upon delivery if the artwork is not in accordance with the brief. If such objection is not received by the Illustrator within 21 days of delivery of artwork it shall be conclusively presumed that the artwork is acceptable.

Approval/Rejection

13. Should the artwork fail to satisfy, the Client may reject the artwork upon payment of a rejection fee as follows:

i. 25% of the agreed fee if the artwork is rejected at the rough stage.

ii. 50% of the agreed fee if the artwork is rejected on delivery.

14. In the event of rejection, ownership of all rights granted under this Agreement shall revert to the Illustrator unless the artwork is based on the Client's visual or otherwise agreed.

Changes

15. If the Client changes the brief and requires subsequent changes, additions or variations, the Illustrator may require additional consideration for such work. The Illustrator may refuse to carry out changes, additions or variations which substantially change the nature of the commission.

Warranties

16. Except where artwork is based on reference material or visuals supplied by the Client or where otherwise agreed, the Illustrator warrants that the artwork is original and does not infringe any existing copyright and further warrants that she/he has not used the artwork elsewhere.

17. The Client warrants that any necessary permissions have been obtained for the agreed use of reference material or visuals supplied by the Client or its customer and shall indemnify the Illustrator against any and all claims and expenses including reasonable legal fees arising from the Illustrator's use of any materials provided by the Client or its customer.

Ownership of Artwork

18. The Illustrator shall retain ownership of all artwork (including roughs and other materials) delivered to the Client.

19. The Illustrator's original artwork shall not be intentionally destroyed, damaged, altered, retouched, modified or changed in any way whatsoever without the written consent of the Illustrator.

20. The Client shall return all artwork to the Illustrator not later than 6 months after delivery in undamaged, unaltered and unretouched condition, although the Client may make and retain scans/files to enable it to exploit the rights granted with the artwork.

A GUIDE TO FINANCE

21. If the artwork is lost or damaged at any time whilst in the Client's custody (which shall mean anytime between delivery of artwork to the Client and its safe return to the Illustrator) the Client shall pay compensation to the Illustrator for the loss/damage of the artwork at a rate to be agreed.

22. The Client shall not be liable for any consequential loss or damages arsing from loss or damage to the artwork.

Credits/Moral Rights

23. The Client shall ensure the Illustrator is credited in any editorial use of the artwork. Credits for non-editorial use are not required unless so indicated on the front of the form.

Samples

24. Unless otherwise agreed, the Illustrator shall be entitled to receive not less than four proofs or printed copies of the work.

Notices

25. All notices shall be sent to the Illustrator and to the Client at the address stated in this Agreement. Each party shall give written notification of any change of address to the other party prior to the date of such change.

Governing Law

26. These terms and conditions are governed by the law of England and Wales and may not be varied except by agreement in writing. The parties hereto submit to the non-exclusive jurisdiction of the English Courts.

Tax

UK: For help with Self Assessment visit www.hmrc.gov.uk/sa or call 0845 900 0444

Newly self-employed visit www.hmrc.gov.uk/startingup or call 0845 915 4515

UK Business Bank account: www.gov.uk/browse/business/setting-up

USA: www.sba.gov/content/5-steps-registering-your-business

Sales tax: A tax on items sold which is determined on an individual state basis. It is of variable amounts. The tax does not apply to services, including the service of transferring reproduction rights.

Collective Licensing

Collective licensing is used in the UK and European countries in situations where it would be difficult for artists and authors to licence the rights they hold in published works, such as books and magazines, on an individual basis. All rights holders are opted into the collective licensing, and it is organized through collective management societies.

- DACS Payback scheme www.dacs.org.uk

- European Visual Artists (EVA) www.evartists.org

Public Lending Right (PLR)

UK: Public Lending Right (PLR) is the right for authors to receive payment under PLR legislation for the loans of their books by public libraries.

www.plr.uk.com

The PLR International Network brings together those countries with established PLR systems: www.plrinternational.com

Canada: www.plr-dpp.ca

A SAMPLE INVOICE

INVOICE

Your name

Address

email address, telephone and website if applicable

Your client's name

Address

Date
(this is really important: as you expect to be paid within a specified time frame)

Invoice number
E.g. JD0001
(make these consecutive)

Client order/Job number
(if appropriate)

Payment *(put a brief description of what was agreed in the licence)*

E.g. 5 illustrations to be used on tea packaging. This use only for 12 months worldwide	**$/ £ XXX** *per illustration*
	Expenses *(if applicable)*
	Taxes *(if applicable/due – Sales Tax in USA, VAT in UK)*
	Total

As agreed

Signed *(by illustrator)*

All payment to be made within 30 days. Any transfer of rights is conditional on receipt of full payment.

USEFUL RESOURCES

COMPETITIONS

American Illustration
www.ai-ap.com

AOI Illustration Awards
www.aoiawards.com

European Design Awards
www.europeandesign.org

Illustration Friday
www.illustrationfriday.com

Society of Illustrators Awards
www.soicompetitions.org

The Big Draw
www.campaignfordrawing.org

Victoria & Albert Museum
IIlustration Awards
http://www.vam.ac.uk

VISIT

Bologna Children's Book Fair
www.bookfair.bolognafiere.it

Brand Licensing
www.brandlicensing.eu

Frankfurt Book Fair
www.frankfurt-book-fair.com

International Book Festival
www.edbookfest.co.uk

Illustrative
www.illustrative.de

ICON
www.theillustrationconference.org

London Book Fair
www.londonbookfair.co.uk

Pictoplasma
www pictoplasma.com

Spring Fair
www.springfair.com

SURTEX
www.surtex.com

ILLUSTRATION WEBSITES

Amelia's Magazine
www.ameliasmagazine.com

Cartoon Brew
www.cartoonbrew.com

Childrens Illustrators
www.childrensillustrators.com

Drawn!
www.drawn.ca

Grain Edit
www.grainedit.com

House of Illustration
www.houseofillustration.org.uk

Illustration Friday
www.illustrationfriday.com

Illustrationmundo
 www.illustrationmundo.com

Little Chimp Society
www.thelittlechimpsociety.com

Vinyl Pulse
www.vinylpulse.com

Urban Sketchers
www.urbansketchers.org

RETAIL WEBSITES

Etsy
www.etsy.com

Not On the High Street
www.notonthehighstreet.com

Society6
www.society6.com

PROMOTIONAL RESOURCES

Adbase
www.adbase.com

AOI client directories
www.theaoi.com

Altpick
altpick.com

Behance Network
www.behance.com

Bikini Lists
www.bikinilists.com

Contact
www.contact-creative.com

Directory of Illustration
www.directoryofillustration.com

Flickr
www.flickr.com

Illoz
www.illoz.com

Linked In
www.linkedin.com

The ispot
www.theispot.com

Twitter
www.twitter.com

ONLINE READING

3x3
www.3x3mag.com

Computer Arts
www.computerarts.co.uk

Communication Arts
www.commarts.com

Creative Review
www.creativereview.co.uk

Eye
www.eyemagazine.com/home.php

Illustration
www.illustration-mag.com

Print
www.printmag.com

Varoom
www.varoom-mag.com

Writers and artists yearbook
www.writersandartists.co.uk

ORGANIZATIONS

AIGA (the professional association for design)
www.aiga.org

Association of Illustrators
www.theaoi.com

D&AD
www.dandad.org

Design and Artist Copyright Society (DACS)
www.dacs.org.uk

European Illustrators Forum (EIF)
www.europeanillustrators.eu

Graphics Artists Guild
www.graphicartistsguild.or

Icograda
www.icograda.org

Illustrators' Partnership
www.illustratorspartnership.org

Society of Children's Book Writers & Illustrators
www.scbwi.org

The Society of Illustrators
www.societyillustrators.org

BOOKS

Rosanne Bell & Angus Hyland
Hand to Eye – Contemporary Illustration
Laurence King Publishing

Laird Borrelli
Fashion Illustration Now
Thames & Hudson, 2004

Derek Brazell & Jo Davies
Making Great Illustration
A&C Black, 2011

Gabriel Campanario
The Art of Urban Sketching: Drawing on Location Around the World
Quarry Books, 2012

Jerelle Kraus
All the Art That's Fit to Print
Columbia University Press, 2012

Tristan Manco
Street Sketchbook
Thames & Hudson, 2010

Simon Stern, AOI
Illustrator's Guide to Law and Business Practice
AOI, 2008

Roger Walton
The Big Book of Illustration Ideas 2
Harper Design International, 2008

Mark Wigan
Basics Illustration: Thinking Visually
AVA Publishing, 2006

Lawrence Zeegen
The Fundamentals of Illustration
AVA Publishing, 2012

CONTRIBUTING ILLUSTRATORS

Rebecca Abell
www.rebeccaabell.co.uk

Gabrielle Adamson
www.gabrielleadamson.co.uk

Gail Armstrong
www.illustrationweb.com/artists/GailArmstrong

Caroline Attia Lariviere
www.carolineattia.com

Evgenia Barinova
www.evgeniabarinova.com

Wesley Bedrosian
www.wesleybedrosian.com

Serge Bloch
www.sergebloch.net

Hartwig Braun
www.hartwigbraun.com

Derek Brazell
www.derekbrazell.com

Paul Buckley
www.flickr.com/photos/paulbuckleydesign

Marc Burckhardt
www.marcart.net

Tom Burns
www.tomburns.co.uk

Tad Carpenter
www.tadcarpenter.com

Lille Carré
www.lillicarre.com

Alberto Cerriteño
www.albertocerriteno.com

Pomme Chan
www.pommepomme.com

Sophia Chang
www.esymai.com

Marcos Chin
www.marcoschin.com

Stephen Collins
www.stephencollinsillustration.com

Jo Davies
www.jodaviesillustration.com

Adolie Day
www.adolieday.blogspot.co.uk

Agnès Decourchelle
www.agnesdecourchelle.blogspot.co.uk

Catalina Estrada
www.catalinaestrada.com

Kate Evans
www.jamaicastreetartists.co.uk/kate.html

Holly Exley
www.hollyexley.com

Yvetta Fedorova
www.scottmenchin.com

Anna-Louise Felstead
www.alfelstead.com

Craig Foster
www.illustrationweb.com/artists/CraigFoster

Daniel Frost
www.danielfrost.co.uk

Karen Greenberg
www.karengreenberg.com

Robin Heighway-Bury
www.robinheighway-bury.com

Steve Hird
www.stevehird.blogspot.co.uk

Jessica Hische
www.jessicahische.is

Rob Hodgson
www.robhodgson.com

Merijn Hos
www.merijnhos.com

Øivind Hovland
www.oivindhovland.com

Daniel Hsieh
www.silvermoon.com

Laura Hughes
www.laurahughes-illustrator.co.uk

Tom Jay
www.tomjay.com

Matt Jones
www.mattjonezanimation.blogspot.co.uk

Michael Kirkham
www.michaelkirkham.com

Stuart Kolakovic
www.stuartkolakovic.co.uk

Gemma Latimer
www.gemmalatimer.com

Libby McMullin
www.misslibby.co.uk

Kanitta Meechubot
www.meechubot.com

Mario Minichiello
www.reportager.uwe.ac.uk/mmini.htm

Chris Moore
www.chrismooreillustration.co.uk

Ben Newman
www.bennewman.co.uk

Hattie Newman
www.hattienewman.co.uk

Zachariah OHora
www.zohora.com

Luke Pearson
www.lukepearson.com

Beth Pountney
www.bethdesign.co.uk

Ulla Pugaard
www.ullapuggaard.com

David Roberts
www.davidrobertsillustration.com

Paolo Rui
www.paolorui.com

Problem Bob
www.problembob.com

Lucinda Rogers
www.lucindarogers.co.uk

Thereza Rowe
www.therezarowe.com

Paul Ryding
www.paulryding.com

Robert Sae-Heng
www.robertsae-heng.co.uk

Natsko Seiki
www.natsko.com

Steve Simpson
www.stevesimpson.com

Lasse Skarbövik
www.lasseskarbovik.com

Mark Smith
www.marksmithillustration.com

Anna Steinberg
www.annasteinberg.co.uk

Peter Strain
www.peterstrain.co.uk

Rachell Sumpter
www.rsumpter.com

Harriet Taylor Seed
www.harrydrawspictures.com

Stephan Walter
www.stephanwalter.ch

Anke Weckmann
www.linotte.net

Ellen Weinstein
www.ellenweinstein.com

Alice Wellinger
www.alice-wellinger.com

Lesley White
www.lesleywhite.co.uk

Stuart Whitton
www.stuartwhitton.co.uk

Zara Wood aka Woody
www.zarawood.com

Olimpia Zagnoli
www.olimpiazagnoli.com

IMAGE CREDITS

CONTRIBUTING AGENTS

Bernstein & Andriulli, USA
www.ba-reps.com

Central Illustration Agency, UK
www.centralillustration.com

Ed Victor literary agents, UK
www.edvictor.com

**The Great British
Card Company, UK**
www.greatbritishcards.co.uk

The Jacky Winter Group, Australia
www.jackywinter.com

Cover image by Steve Simpson

P7 Stuart Kolakovic

P9 Holly Exley

P11 Gemma Latimer

P12 Lasse Skarbövik

P13 Daniel Hsieh for Locus Publishing

P14 Pomme Chan,
www.pommepomme.com

P15 Wesley Bedrosian

P16 Paul Blow

P17 Fig.6 Chris Moore for Orion

P17 Fig.7 Tom Burns

P18 David Roberts, Uncle Montague's
Tales of Terror by Chris Priestley,
Bloomsbury Publishing, 2007

P19 Luke Pearson for Nobrow Press

P20 Fig.10 Copyright Anke Weckmann

P20 Fig.11 Stuart Kolakovic

P21 Fig 12 Ulla Puggaard

P21 Fig.13 Karen Greenberg, Landor
Associates, Kraft Foods

P22/23 Problem Bob

P24/25 Matt Jones/Pixar

P26 Evolution Studios / Sony

P27 Lucinda Rogers

P28 Alberto Cerriteño

P29 Catalina Estrada, Joumma Bags

P30 Fig.27 Evgenia Barinova

P30 Fig.28 Lilli Carré

P31 Agnes Decourchelle

P33 Marcos Chin

P34 Olimpia Zagnoli

P37 Alberto Cerriteño

P39 Paolo Rui

P41 Ben Newman

P45 Ashley Potter

P47 Thereza Rowe

P50 Paul Buckley

P51 Anna Steinberg

P52 Rob Hodgson

P53 Stephan Walter

P56/57 Woody

P61 Anna-Louise Felsted

P63 Matt Taylor, Rachell Sumpter

P65 Gabrielle Adamson

P67 Øivind Hovland

P69 All illustrations by Peter Strain.
All images are copyrighted by the
artist

P71 Daniel Frost Fig.1 Photograph
by Sam Hofman and YCM, Fig.2
Photograph by Guy Archard and YCN.

P72 Fig.3 Problem Bob

P72 Fig.4 Evgenia Baranova

P73 Natsko Seki

P75 Marc Burckhardt, Hattie Newman,
Serge Bloch

P77 Pomme Chan

P79 Jack Teagle

P85 Merijn Hos

P86 www.surtex.com

P87 Stuart Whitton

Many thanks to all the illustrators, agents and commissioners who generously contributed to *Becoming a Successful Illustrator*; those who gave their time to expand on their professional experience and advice and also allowed use of their images to accompany their quotes or case studies, as well as Steve, Kanitta, Gemma, Øivind, Thereza, Rob and Robert who created bespoke illustrations for the chapter headings and cover.

Much of the content here has evolved directly from the lessons we both learned from Simon Stern (1943–2009), to whom we are indebted for his exemplary training in the ethical aspects of illustration. He gave us knowledge which has taken us forward through our careers, allowing us to pass on essential information to students and Association of Illustrators members. He's still missed.

The Illustration team at Plymouth University, headed by Ashley Potter have developed enterprise modules that have expanded an understanding of what students need for success in the profession. Their excellence as tutors and the responsiveness of undergraduate students is reflected in this book. Jo benefitted from support for research from Message research group and Plymouth University.

Thanks to the Association of Illustrators, our editor at AVA, Leafy Cummins, and all our family and friends for their support.

All the organizations and companies whose commissions are published in the book, including:

Entertainment One for supplying images from *A Monster In Paris*, Bibo Films, 2011.

Evolution Studios/Sony for *MotorStorm Apocalypse*, signs and logos copyright of Sony and Evolution Studios, 2010.

And to all our readers, we wish you the best of luck in your illustration careers. Keep on drawing...and aim high.

The publisher would like to thank Mark Boardman, Alaiyo Bradshaw, Chris Draper, Nora Krug and Louis Netter for their reviews of the manuscript.